CAREC GENDER STRATEGY 2030
INCLUSION, EMPOWERMENT, AND RESILIENCE FOR ALL

JANUARY 2021

Notes:
In this publication, "$" refers to United States dollars.
ADB recognizes "China" as the People's Republic of China.

Cover design by Jasper Lauzon.

On the cover: Women and girls in CAREC member countries (photos by ADB Photo Library).

CONTENTS

TABLES

ABBREVIATIONS

ADB	Asian Development Bank
CAREC	Central Asia Regional Economic Cooperation
COVID-19	coronavirus disease
GII	Gender Inequality Index
ICT	information and communication technology
MSMEs	micro, small, and medium-sized enterprises
NFP	national focal point
NGO	nongovernment organization
PRC	People's Republic of China
RGEG	Regional Gender Expert Group
SDG	Sustainable Development Goal
STEM	science, technology, engineering, and mathematics
TVET	technical and vocational education and training
UN	United Nations
UNDP	United Nations Development Programme

EXECUTIVE SUMMARY

INTRODUCTION

The Central Asia Regional Economic Cooperation (CAREC) Gender Strategy 2030 is intended to complement CAREC 2030, providing strategic guidelines for mainstreaming gender into CAREC's five operational clusters: (i) economic and financial stability; (ii) trade, tourism, and economic corridors; (iii) infrastructure and economic connectivity; (iv) agriculture and water; and (v) human development. The CAREC Gender Strategy 2030 draws on findings and insights from a comprehensive CAREC Gender Assessment of the program's operations conducted in 2019, which is available on demand through the CAREC Secretariat.

RATIONALE AND PURPOSE OF THE CAREC GENDER STRATEGY 2030

The purpose of this strategy is to increase the potential and capacity of women in the participating countries to benefit equally from CAREC investments and interventions, and to have equal access to any opportunities created through the regional cooperation mechanism. To these ends, implementation of CAREC 2030 requires the active participation of women and men living in the CAREC countries, and targeted efforts to promote gender equality and reduce gender disparities. A regional strategy that supports equalization of opportunities for women and men is needed for the following reasons:

- **CAREC countries have several common challenges and bottlenecks to improving the quality of lives of women.** There is a systemic gender gap in labor force participation across all CAREC countries, with disparities in employment rates, pay scales, and quality of employment.

There are also common gender biases in hiring practices and promotion opportunities, and failures to implement national policies on flexible working arrangements, parental leave, and equal pay. In many countries, female entrepreneurship is undermined by factors that include lack of finances for start-ups and expansion because of women's limited ownership of assets to leverage credit. Women's political participation in all CAREC countries falls well below 33%, and the proportion of women in senior management positions remains low. Women in the region are also often among the most affected by external shocks, such as drought or flooding, linked to climate change; food and oil price fluctuations; and global pandemics, such as the coronavirus disease (COVID-19), because of their disproportionate exposure to risk and increased pressure to undertake primary care responsibilities.

- **CAREC countries can learn from each other on strengthening their national approaches on gender mainstreaming.** Gender equality and women's empowerment are necessary preconditions of economic growth and inclusive, equitable, and sustainable development. Empowering women as active participants in development makes good economic sense and is associated with reduced poverty, faster growth, and concomitant benefits for society. As CAREC countries face common challenges, knowledge sharing on best practices and lessons learned among member countries can help strengthen their national strategies on gender mainstreaming to meet these preconditions and achieve gender equality and women's empowerment.

- **Opportunities have been missed to mainstream gender effectively across regional projects supported under CAREC.** There are gaps and missed opportunities with regard to the integration of gender equality in CAREC-assisted projects. The CAREC Gender Assessment shows that only 9.4% of the analyzed CAREC projects (10 of 107) achieved an *effective gender mainstreaming* Asian Development Bank (ADB) category, while 25% (26 of 107) achieved *some gender elements* ADB category. Gender mainstreaming has been limited in the energy and transport projects. There is, therefore, a clear need for a gender strategy that sets out clear entry points for gender-responsive planning and implementation.

- **Regional support under CAREC can add value to national efforts and programs for gender.** A regional approach to gender mainstreaming taken through the CAREC Gender Strategy 2030 can complement national actions and existing programs to support women's empowerment in the region.

- **All CAREC countries have committed to the Sustainable Development Goals and to key international gender equality agreements.** All CAREC countries are signatories of the Sustainable Development Goals (SDGs). This represents a common commitment to prioritize gender equality and women's empowerment in national development agendas and to integrate these considerations through actions relating to the achievement of all 17 SDGs. All CAREC countries have ratified the Convention on the Elimination of All Forms of Discrimination against Women; are signatories of the Beijing Platform for Action; and, as United Nations (UN) member states, have a responsibility to implement the UN Security Council Resolution 1325 on women, peace, and security.

- **CAREC development partners are committed to advancing gender equality and empowering women.** Key CAREC partner organizations, such as ADB, the Asian Infrastructure Investment Bank, the European Bank for Reconstruction and Development, the International Monetary Fund, the Islamic Development Bank, the United Nations Development Programme, and the World Bank all view gender equality and women's empowerment as key drivers of economic growth and social development.

CAREC GENDER STRATEGY APPROACH AND FRAMEWORK

The vision of the CAREC Gender Strategy is "*inclusion, empowerment, and resilience for all.*" Regional and intercountry support under CAREC is designed to strengthen and complement national strategies and programs for women's empowerment and gender mainstreaming. This reflects the critical need for additional efforts that ensure the inclusion of women's specific needs and voices at all stages of planning and implementation in regional projects; to promote the empowerment of women through access to capacity building, economic opportunities, and involvement in decision-making; and to contribute to greater resilience for women and their families to minimize risk, promote well-being, and enable sustainable, gender-equitable outcomes. To achieve this vision, the proposed mission is "*equality and empowerment of women and girls in all CAREC operations for inclusive, shared, and sustainable development.*"

The broad objectives of the strategy, designed to achieve this mission, are as follows:

Objective 1: Promote women's access to economic opportunities. Where possible, CAREC interventions will be designed to supplement and add value to national efforts to create opportunities for women to enter paid and formal employment in relevant sectors, support women in agriculture and informal sectors, promote women's entrepreneurship, and enable women to gain skills that prepare them for jobs and business opportunities in the CAREC sectors.

Objective 2: Contribute to women's social empowerment. CAREC interventions will include regional provisions that combine with national strategies to advance gender equality and women's empowerment in terms of (a) enhancing women's decision-making roles; (b) reducing women's time poverty; (c) taking into account specific needs and concerns of women and girls through projects' consultative processes; (d) promoting women's safety, resilience, and security; and (e) strengthening human capital development across the CAREC countries in education by connecting women to regional institutes of higher education and centers of excellence, and in health by connecting them to regionwide quality healthcare services and providing access to tertiary hospitals and specialized treatment institutions.

Objective 3: Support women's regional networks and policy reform for women's empowerment. CAREC will support gender-responsive policy reforms where current legislation is exacerbating gender disparities and creating barriers to women's economic empowerment; it will also contribute to an enabling environment for fostering knowledge sharing. Regional networks of women will be supported (a) to allow exchange of information across borders on legislative and regulatory regimes for women's empowerment in the various CAREC countries, and (b) to enhance access to information about income-earning and social development opportunities across the region.

Objective 4: Enhance women's access to information and communication technology. CAREC interventions will promote better regional digital connectivity by enhancing access of women and men to, and training in, new digital technologies and affordable information and communication technology (ICT) solutions. Such interventions will reduce the connectivity costs across borders and countries, improve competitiveness of small firms and businesses that employ women, and reduce social progress gaps between men and women in the CAREC region.

MAINSTREAMING GENDER INTO CAREC OPERATIONAL CLUSTERS

Key gender issues and potential strategic directions and entry points for gender mainstreaming through CAREC's five operational clusters are outlined in this chapter. Additional guidelines are also provided for ICT, which is a crosscutting theme under CAREC 2030. A full list of strategic gender entry points is available in the attached Appendix. Due to the socioeconomic and cultural diversity of the CAREC countries, decisions will need to be made regarding the prioritization of entry points in individual countries, while the selected entry points will need to be adapted and refined for each country context.

Economic and Financial Stability Cluster

Women and men often do not benefit equally from economic growth and fiscal measures designed to boost economies. This is true of the CAREC region where, in all countries, there is a clear gender pay gap, and women often face discrimination in recruitment and employment practices. Gender inequalities also often prevent existing and potential female entrepreneurs from accessing credit and the financial products, services, and information that could help them start or scale up micro, small, and medium-sized enterprises.

CAREC will ensure that operations within this cluster promote equal opportunities for women, including in nontraditional jobs and management in both private and public sectors, and promote the creation of an enabling environment for female entrepreneurs so that they can take full advantage of national programs and new regional economic opportunities in the productive and services sectors. To ensure effective gender-responsive planning and implementation, CAREC will promote policy dialogue at regional and cross-country levels to enable stakeholders from across the region to learn from each other's experiences and knowledge and put in place best practices for women's empowerment and gender mainstreaming. CAREC initiatives will seek to work with and support the banking and private sectors at the regional levels that promote financial inclusion and economic empowerment of women.

Trade, Tourism, and Economic Corridors Cluster

Trade

Informal, small-scale, cross-border trading activities across the CAREC countries are a major source of income for many women. CAREC, in alignment with the CAREC Integrated Trade Agenda 2030, will support initiatives aiming at removing supply chain barriers, particularly those that inhibit women entrepreneurs in the region. CAREC can also consider providing support to member countries for the revision of national and regional trade policies to include gender-responsive measures and will facilitate consultations with female traders across borders for this purpose. CAREC will also enhance information sharing and provide appropriate training for border officials to minimize discrimination by gender.

Tourism

Tourism also offers many potential opportunities for women, including decent work, entrepreneurship, and leadership roles. CAREC, in alignment with the CAREC Tourism Strategy 2030, will promote initiatives to ensure women have equal access to information about tourism-related jobs across the region and will provide support to the countries to develop regional and cross-country guidelines to ensure nondiscriminatory recruitment and equal pay and access to opportunities. CAREC will actively engage both women and men from local communities, including those in the border areas, in the planning, development, and implementation of tourist attractions and related services. Regional capacity building programs will focus on skills building of both women and men regional tourism operators and on private sector tourism businesses to ensure inclusive corporate policies.

Economic Corridors

Economic corridors in the CAREC region provide an effective tool to create business development opportunities, employment, and entrepreneurship, promoting growth through deepened regional cooperation and integration. Through existing CAREC initiatives, such as the Almaty–Bishkek Economic Corridor and the Trilateral Economic Corridor connecting Kazakhstan, Uzbekistan, and Tajikistan, the CAREC Program will promote initiatives to increase women participation in cross-border trade, tourism-related services, agricultural regional value chain, integrated urban planning, and knowledge-sharing and training events.

Infrastructure and Economic Connectivity Cluster

Transport

There are often significant gender differences in transport usage and trip patterns in CAREC countries. For example, women in CAREC countries are less likely to drive and own a vehicle than men. Constraints that include cost, lack of provision, and inconvenience prevent many women from using public transport in the CAREC countries. Another key issue is safety—sexual harassment on public transport has been reported as a growing problem in many CAREC countries. Walking is, therefore, the primary mode of travel for many women, yet roads are often not designed with pedestrians in mind.

CAREC, in alignment with the CAREC Transport Strategy 2030, will ensure that regional roads and railways, and public transport services connecting countries are designed in ways that prioritize affordability, convenience, accessibility, and safety for all women and children. CAREC will provide support for collecting gender-disaggregated data for the development of inclusive regional solutions. CAREC will provide trainings to transport service providers at regional level in raising awareness on protecting women from sexual and other forms of harassment, aiming at the development of zero-tolerance policies and effective reporting mechanisms, as well as facilitate the establishment of regional information and exchange networks. CAREC will support member countries in developing regional policies and guidelines to ensure the employment potential of women in the transport sector is harnessed.

Energy

Access to a clean and modern energy supply can have improved health and well-being outcomes as well as implications for economic empowerment across the CAREC region, freeing up time for women, which would otherwise be spent seeking fuel for cooking and domestic heating. The energy sector could likewise provide a useful source of employment for women, particularly in the growing sustainable energy market.

The CAREC Energy Strategy 2030 includes "Empowering Women in Energy" as a crosscutting theme. To increase women's visibility in the sector, the strategy foresees the establishment of a regional women's energy program to improve their careers and make them more employable. Setting up regional networking and support facilities is also envisioned. To complement these initiatives, the CAREC Gender Strategy will seek to strengthen and inform regional energy policies focused on fostering equal opportunities for women and men and on reducing domestic energy costs that are of particular benefit to women. CAREC will actively support initiatives to create women's employment in the growing green energy market at the regional level. CAREC will also enable regional partnerships between regional energy suppliers, universities, and technical and vocational education and training (TVET) institutions to provide professional development for women in energy-related operations.

Agriculture and Water Cluster

Agriculture

Many women in the CAREC countries work in agriculture, reaching up to 82% of the economically active women in countries such as Afghanistan. However, this work is poorly paid or even unpaid. Women farmers face challenges that include limited access to productive resources such as land, water, seeds, and labor-saving tools; and to higher-value markets and information. Closing the gender gap in agriculture requires multiple actions at the policy and practical levels.

To do so, CAREC will promote the development of both regional and country-level approaches to promote equitable access to water, credit, agricultural extension services, and digital technologies. Ongoing activities conducted by CAREC in the agriculture sector include (i) training and participation of women in sanitary and phytosanitary safeguards and standards to promote better safety standards, including through the establishment of a regional food safety network; and (ii) development of regional wholesale markets, which will provide bigger avenues for women farmers to market their produce and earn additional incomes through engaging in cross-border trade. The CAREC Gender Strategy 2030 will complement these activities and strengthen gender mainstreaming through, for example, capacity building for women farmers on new agricultural practices and technologies, which will contribute to create regional agricultural value chains.

Water Management

In the CAREC countries, women often have the primary responsibility for water management of the household and are thus disproportionately burdened by water supply and quality issues. They are also significantly impacted by flooding and waterborne diseases. In addition, women in the CAREC countries have limited representation in water user associations, partly because inequitable laws prevent them from being registered as landowners.

CAREC will facilitate women's participation in regional mechanisms for transboundary water resource management. It will also increase their representation in regional emergency responses to address impacts on food and water security and on water and sanitation infrastructure. CAREC can also consider providing support to establish mechanisms to recruit women into technical and managerial roles in the water sector and to provide on-the-job trainings for them to participate more effectively in regional water projects.

Human Development

Education

The majority of CAREC countries have achieved gender parity or near parity in primary and secondary education. However, women still lag far behind in science, technology, engineering, and mathematics (STEM) subjects. Although women account for the majority of teachers in many CAREC countries, they are not well represented in higher-level decision-making posts in educational establishments.

In strengthening human capital development in education across member countries, CAREC will help to connect women of the region to institutes of higher education and technical training to boost their education status and increase their income-earning capacities. To do so, CAREC will support the development of strategies at the regional and intercountry levels that could include partnering with national and regional TVET providers to offer trainings in nontraditional subjects, including STEM, and technical skills such as plumbing, carpentry, and electrical work among girls and young women. CAREC will also promote regional efforts to increase women's representation in the management of educational institutions.

Health

There has been a steady improvement across health indicators in the CAREC countries, but there is continued poor access to health services in some countries, particularly those with low or medium ranking in UNDP's Human Development Index. It is also likely that several gains in health sector improvement in the CAREC countries will have been undermined by the global COVID-19 pandemic.

In response, CAREC will support countries in developing a regional health strategy that will, among other things, strengthen surveillance systems and monitoring capabilities across borders for control of communicable and noncommunicable diseases, and improve access of women and men to quality medicines at more affordable costs across the region. CAREC will also facilitate knowledge sharing on new technologies, such as cross-border telemedicine and access to medical support across the region. This will enhance access to quality health services, particularly for women who have limited mobility and constrained access to medical advice.

Information and Communication Technology

The importance of digital technology is becoming increasingly evident across the world, particularly in light of the COVID-19 pandemic. ICT is providing an invaluable resource for businesses in the form of e-commerce and virtual communications as well as for access to education, health, and other vital services. This makes it vital to address the digital divide in many CAREC countries, where women lag behind men in access to digital technology. For example, there are disparities between male and female phone ownership and mobile internet usage in the region. This means that women are unable to participate in new forms of economic activity that rely on digital platforms and ICT.

To help close this gender gap in digital access, CAREC will support capacity building in ICT for women and girls of all ages through regional trainings and workshops. CAREC will also seek engagement with private sector ICT companies to facilitate the provision of internet access, especially for women in poor households. In addition, CAREC will promote the creation of regional knowledge networks to share good, gender-sensitive practices for enhancing women's access to ICT and increasing their opportunities in information technology-related employment.

INSTITUTIONAL ARRANGEMENTS

The CAREC Gender Strategy 2030 will supplement and add value to the CAREC countries' national efforts and strategies on gender to best achieve women's empowerment in the region. It will be implemented through the CAREC sector strategies and action plans. The CAREC Secretariat will coordinate the implementation of the Gender Strategy 2030.

Three institutional arrangements, aligned with the CAREC 2030 Institutional Framework, will be established: (i) a CAREC Regional Gender Expert Group (RGEG) that will provide strategic guidance and expert inputs, as and where needed, for the strategy's effective implementation; (ii) enhanced collaboration between the CAREC Secretariat, member countries, development partners, and the CAREC Institute, which will ensure collaboration, knowledge sharing, and mutual learning; and (iii) a monitoring and evaluation mechanism, which will facilitate tracking and communication of results across the CAREC region on the implementation of the CAREC Gender Strategy.

CAREC GENDER STRATEGY 2030 RESULTS FRAMEWORK

A results framework is provided, which demonstrates the results chain, stating expected outputs and the desired outcomes for each operational cluster and for each defined objective. The projected outcomes and outputs will contribute to the overall impact of inclusion, empowerment, and resilience for all in the CAREC region. The results framework will help member countries and the CAREC Secretariat monitor progress of the CAREC Gender Strategy 2030. The CAREC Secretariat will closely work with the sector committees, working groups, and proposed RGEG to feed sector strategies into this mechanism and develop concrete cluster and sector-specific indicators.

CHAPTER I

INTRODUCTION

1.   The Central Asia Regional Economic Cooperation (CAREC) Program is a partnership of 11 member countries[1] and development partners[2] working together to promote development through cooperation, leading to accelerated economic growth and poverty reduction. It is guided by the overarching vision of "good neighbors, good partners, and good prospects" and its mission of creating an "open and inclusive platform for regional cooperation to connect people, policies, and projects for shared and sustainable development."[3]

2.   Regional actions under CAREC are designed to complement and support the delivery of country-level priorities set out in national strategies and development plans, and of global-wide objectives articulated through the Sustainable Development Goals (SDGs) and the 21st Conference of the Parties (COP21) to the United Nations Framework Convention on Climate Change global climate agreement.

3.   In October 2017, the CAREC Program entered a new period of cooperation following the adoption of the CAREC 2030 Strategic Framework. Operational priorities under the CAREC 2030 strategy fall into five primary clusters: (i) economic and financial stability; (ii) trade, tourism, and economic corridors; (iii) infrastructure and economic connectivity; (iv) agriculture and water;

and (v) human development; while integrating the use of information and communication technology (ICT), gender mainstreaming, and climate change mitigation are crosscutting priorities. The CAREC Institute facilitates knowledge sharing as well as building capacity and providing training for stakeholders from member countries.

4.   CAREC member countries are committed to implementing the CAREC 2030 vision in a gender-responsive and gender-sensitive manner. There is consensus on the importance of gender mainstreaming in CAREC to help achieve increased economic growth, inclusive social development, and SDGs. This imperative has become more urgent in light of the global coronavirus disease (COVID-19) pandemic, which has had disproportionate effects on women. Women's unpaid care work has increased significantly because of school closures and the increased needs of older people. The virus has also impacted women harder as they often work in insecure labor markets or in the informal economy, which further increases their vulnerabilities towards economic shocks. Furthermore, violence against women and girls has also intensified due to lockdown measures. Consequently, progress made in the region towards gender equality and women's empowerment could experience serious setback due to the COVID-19 pandemic.[4]

---

[1]   The CAREC member countries are Afghanistan, Azerbaijan, the People's Republic of China (PRC), Georgia, Kazakhstan, the Kyrgyz Republic, Mongolia, Pakistan, Tajikistan, Turkmenistan, and Uzbekistan.

[2]   Six multilateral financial institutions have been part of CAREC since its early years: Asian Development Bank (ADB), European Bank for Reconstruction and Development (EBRD), International Monetary Fund (IMF), Islamic Development Bank (IsDB), United Nations Development Programme (UNDP), and the World Bank. New development partners, including the Asian Infrastructure Investment Bank (AIIB), and others are joining.

[3]   ADB. 2017. *CAREC 2030: Connecting the Region for Shared and Sustainable Development*. Manila.

[4]   United Nations. 2020. *Policy Brief: The Impact of COVID-19 on Women*. New York. 9 April.

5.   The purpose of the CAREC Gender Strategy is to complement CAREC 2030, providing strategic guidelines for mainstreaming gender into the five operational clusters. The strategy draws on findings and insights from a comprehensive gender assessment of CAREC operations conducted in 2019.[5] Chapter II sets out a rationale for the strategy, articulating the added socioeconomic value of mainstreaming gender across the five clusters in the CAREC countries. Chapter III defines the CAREC Gender Strategy regional approach including vision, mission, and objectives. Chapter IV provides strategic entry points and suggested actions for mainstreaming gender across CAREC interventions, with more detailed potential actions in the attached Appendix. The entry points fall under four key objectives, achievement of which will enable progress towards the mission and overall vision for the strategy. Chapter V includes specific recommendations on institutional arrangements for the CAREC Secretariat to ensure implementation of the strategy. Finally, Chapter VI includes a results framework that demonstrates the results chain, leading from the CAREC interventions to the expected outputs, and the targeted outcomes in each operational cluster.

---

[5]   The CAREC Gender Assessment provides a diagnostic framework to analyze the gender situation in the 11 CAREC countries. For that, a total of 107 projects implemented by CAREC and other development partners from 2014 to 2018 were reviewed. The assessment followed a mixed methods approach involving a desk review, supplemented by country visits to Azerbaijan, Kazakhstan, and Uzbekistan, where interviews of key informants were conducted. The CAREC Gender Assessment served as basis and major inputs for the formulation of the CAREC Gender Strategy. The CAREC Gender Assessment is available on demand through the CAREC Secretariat.

CHAPTER II

RATIONALE AND PURPOSE OF THE CAREC GENDER STRATEGY 2030

6. The purpose of the CAREC Gender Strategy 2030 is to increase the potential and capacity of women in the participating countries to benefit equally from CAREC investments and interventions and to have equal access to any opportunities created through the regional cooperation mechanism, reflecting CAREC 2030's commitment to inclusive social development. To these ends, implementation of CAREC 2030 requires active participation of both women and men living in the CAREC countries, and targeted efforts to promote gender equality and reduce gender disparities. A regional strategy that supports equalization of opportunities for women and men is needed for reasons discussed in the following sections.

■ CAREC countries share common challenges and bottlenecks to improving the quality of lives of women.

7. In the majority of CAREC countries, women and men have equal rights under the law, including equal rights to access social services. However, recent evidence points to persistent gender-based disparities across multiple indexes in all CAREC countries, particularly in terms of economic empowerment and political representation. According to the 2019 United Nations Development Programme (UNDP) Gender Inequality Index (GII),[6] seven CAREC countries fall into the lowest two-thirds of 189 countries, with only the People's Republic of China (PRC), Kazakhstan, and Uzbekistan ranking in the top one-third (Table 1).[7]

Table 1: United Nations Development Programme 2019 Gender Inequality Index Ranking for Central Asia Regional Economic Cooperation Countries

Country	Ranking
People's Republic of China	39
Kazakhstan	46
Uzbekistan	64
Azerbaijan	70
Mongolia	71
Georgia	75
Tajikistan	84
Kyrgyz Republic	87
Pakistan	136
Afghanistan	143

Note: There is no overall ranking for Turkmenistan in the Gender Inequality Index.

Source: United Nations Development Programme. Human Development Reports. Gender Inequality Index (accessed 2 March 2020).

8. Through effective planning and implementation across its five operational clusters, CAREC has an opportunity to address specific gender inequalities in and across the CAREC countries. The ways and extent to which gender inequalities manifest often vary considerably due to the diverse socioeconomic conditions and cultural norms across the CAREC countries. However, there are some clear regional trends, as outlined below.

---

[6] The GII provides a composite score based on gender parity in education and labor markets, maternal and adolescent mortality rates, and women's parliamentary representation.
[7] UNDP. Human Development Reports. Gender Inequality Index (accessed 2 March 2020).

(i) Women's Economic Empowerment

9.   Women in the CAREC countries face challenges in accessing quality employment. The GII reveals a systemic gender gap in labor force participation across all the CAREC countries, with disparities in employment rates, pay scales, and quality of employment. Economic participation of women is relatively low compared with men in all of the countries, with a particularly wide gap in Pakistan where only 23.9% of working-age women participate in the labor market compared with 81.5% of men (footnote 5).

10.   Data indicate that women in the CAREC countries tend to be concentrated in lower paid and informal sector economic activities, whereas men predominate in well-paid sectors. This translates into lower wages and offers fewer social security benefits than the formal sector. For example, in Kazakhstan, 71.4% of women are employed in the services sector as opposed to 52.0% of men.[8] In the Kyrgyz Republic, 83.6% of the low-paid health and social services workforce is female, while men account for 84.4% of employees in the higher-paid mining industry.[9] This is contributing to a significant gender wage gap in many CAREC countries. For example, women in Georgia earned, on average, 64% of male earnings in 2017.[10] Evidence indicates that the low-paid industries, where many female employees are concentrated, have been badly affected by the impacts of the COVID-19 crisis (footnote 4).

11.   Women entering the paid labor market in the CAREC countries are more likely than men to encounter poor workplace equality standards. Available research and evidence gathered for the Asian Development Bank (ADB) country gender assessments of the CAREC countries point to common gender biases in hiring practices and promotion opportunities, and failures to implement national policies on paid maternity and paternity leave, flexible working arrangements, and equal pay. High rates of sexual harassment and abuse in workplaces have also been reported by female employees in the CAREC countries.[11] However, due to the sensitive nature of these cases, they often go unreported; hence, there are gaps in data.

12.   Micro, small, and medium-sized enterprises (MSMEs) offer opportunities for women to work in flexible ways that fit with their other responsibilities.[12] However, access to finance remains a key challenge for female entrepreneurs across the world. Women also find social and financial difficulties in setting up and running a business. The estimated 80% of women-owned businesses globally with credit needs are either entirely without service or underserved, translating into a financing gap worth $1.7 trillion.[13] There are two major reasons for this gap: (i) women are less invested in the formal banking system, and (ii) women often lack access to assets to fulfil the requirement of collateral for obtaining finance. For example, data collected by ADB shows that women in the Kyrgyz Republic comprised less than half of all borrowers in partner banks, and loans for female borrowers accounted for only 25%–43% of their total portfolio.[14]

---

[8]   ADB. 2018. *Kazakhstan: Country Gender Assessment*. Manila.

[9]   ADB. 2019. *Kyrgyz Republic: Country Gender Assessment*. Manila.

[10] ADB. 2018. *Georgia: Country Gender Assessment*. Manila.

[11] For example, a study conducted by the Mongolian Gender Equality Center (MGEC) in 2004 revealed that one in five women had experienced sexual harassment and that one in three knew someone who had been harassed. A follow-up study in 2017 showed that little had changed and indicated that harassment is often perpetrated by men in positions of power or authority in the workplace (MGEC. 2017. *General Situations and Attitudes on Sexual Harassment Intimidation and Abuse against Women and Girls in the Workplace: Comparative Analysis 2004 and 2017*. Ulaanbaatar).

[12] ADB. 2014. *Gender Tool Kit: Micro, Small, and Medium-Sized Enterprise Finance and Development*. Manila.

[13] International Finance Corporation. 2017. *MSME Finance Gap: Assessment of the Shortfalls and Opportunities in Financing Micro, Small, and Medium Enterprises in Emerging Markets*. Washington, DC.

[14] Data collected in 2017 by ADB on the Kyrgyz Republic (ADB. 2017. Project Report: Consolidated Report on Gender Expertise of PFIs under ADB Women's Entrepreneurship Development Project. Manila).

(ii) Women's Time Poverty

13.   The limited childcare and eldercare institutions and the fact that women across most CAREC countries continue to do the majority of housework and are the primary caregivers, make it difficult for them to balance career and family. In Central Asian countries, women spend between 1.5 and four times as much time as men on unpaid work, with the gap being the lowest in Kazakhstan and highest in Uzbekistan.[15] Similar patterns are prevalent in Azerbaijan, with women spending three times more time on unpaid work compared to men. The withdrawal of state-subsidized childcare in countries such as Mongolia, Georgia, Tajikistan, and the Kyrgyz Republic has been a contributing factor in women's declining participation in the labor market (footnotes 9 and 10). The COVID-19 pandemic has intensified pressure on many women to perform unpaid care work due to the closure of childcare facilities and schools (footnote 4).

(iii) Women's Decision-Making and Leadership

14.   All 11 CAREC countries fare poorly in terms of the proportion of women in managerial positions, ranging from less than 10% of female senior managers in Azerbaijan, Afghanistan, Pakistan, and Tajikistan to over 60% in the PRC.[16] At the national level, women's political participation in all CAREC countries falls well below the 33% advocated by the Beijing Platform for Action:[17] Afghanistan has the highest female representation of all the countries, at 27% of seats in parliament. The lowest female representation is in Georgia, at only 16.0% of seats, closely followed by Azerbaijan and Uzbekistan (16.8%) and Mongolia (17.1%) (footnote 7).

(iv) Women's Vulnerability to External Shocks

15.   External shocks (such as drought or flooding linked to climate change), food and oil price fluctuations, and global pandemics (such as the COVID-19) often affect the poorest and most vulnerable populations in the CAREC countries because of their disproportionate exposure to risk. For example, climate change can compound women's time burden because of the need to travel further for water and fuel in the face of increasingly depleted water reservoirs and scarce forestry resources. Women may also face reduced economic opportunities as sources of employment and income such as agriculture, forests, and rivers are compromised.[18] Women farmers are often among the worst affected because they lack resources and assets to offset the impacts of natural disasters.

(v) Gender Inequitable Access to Information and Communication Technology

16.   CAREC 2030 recognizes the critical importance of closing the digital divide in and between member countries. Even within countries, there are disparities between male and female phone ownership and mobile internet usage. While in some CAREC countries, such as Pakistan, the gender gap in digital access is particularly wide, with only 11% of women being mobile internet users compared with 38% of men, in the PRC and Kazakhstan, there is near gender parity in mobile internet usage.[19] Also, with the exception of the PRC and Kazakhstan, the quality of digital services (bandwidth) is poor in all CAREC countries and the cost of access is high.[20]

[15]   T. Khitarishvili. 2016. *Gender and Employment in South Caucasus and Western CIS*. New York: UNDP.

[16]   World Bank. Enterprise Surveys (accessed August 2020).

[17]   The Beijing Declaration and Platform for Action was endorsed at the 4th World Conference on Women of the UN in Beijing, PRC in 1995. It is considered the most comprehensive global policy framework for the rights of women. It recognizes women's rights as human rights and lays out a roadmap for achieving gender equality, including specific measures and outcomes across issues affecting women and girls (UN Women. The Beijing Platform for Action Turns 20 [accessed 2 March 2020]).

[18]   E. Skinner. 2011. *Gender and Climate Change: Overview Report*. BRIDGE Cutting Edge Pack on Gender and Climate Change. Brighton: Institute of Development Studies (IDS); and A. Brody, J. Demetriades, and E. Esplen. 2008. *Gender and Climate Change: Mapping the Linkages – A Scoping Study on Knowledge and Gaps*. Brighton: BRIDGE/IDS.

[19]   GSMA (Global System for Mobile Communications Association, originally Groupe Spécial Mobile). 2019. *Connected Women: The Mobile Gender Gap Report 2019*. London.

[20]   ADB. 2014. *Information and Communication Technologies for Women Entrepreneurs: Prospects and Potential in Azerbaijan, Kazakhstan, the Kyrgyz Republic, and Uzbekistan*. Manila.

■ **CAREC countries can learn from each other on strengthening their national approaches on gender mainstreaming.**

17.   Gender equality and women's empowerment are necessary preconditions of economic growth and inclusive, equitable, and sustainable development. Empowering women as active participants in development makes good economic sense and is linked with reduced poverty, faster growth, and associated benefits for society. As the CAREC countries face common challenges, knowledge sharing on best practices and lessons learned among member countries can help strengthen their national strategies on gender mainstreaming to meet these preconditions and achieve gender equality and women's empowerment.

18.   Conversely, if women are not enabled to achieve their full economic potential, growth and poverty reduction will be significantly undermined, with other negative implications such as less favorable education and health outcomes for children.

■ **Opportunities have been missed to mainstream gender effectively across regional projects supported under CAREC.**

19.   The 2019 gender assessment of CAREC indicates some good, gender-sensitive practices and policies, but there are also gaps and missed opportunities in CAREC-assisted projects. This gender assessment shows that only 9.4% of the analyzed CAREC projects (10 of 107) achieved an *effective gender mainstreaming*

ADB category, while 25.0% (26 of 107) achieved *some gender elements* ADB category.[21] In particular, gender mainstreaming has been limited in energy and transport projects—between 2014 and 2018, out of the analyzed sample, 10 of 16 energy projects and 28 of 59 transport projects were classified as having *no gender elements*. There is, therefore, a clear need for a CAREC gender strategy articulating good practices and setting out entry points for planning and implementation.

■ **Regional support under CAREC can add value to national efforts and programs for gender.**

20.   A regional approach to gender mainstreaming taken through the CAREC Gender Strategy 2030 can complement national actions and existing programs to support women's empowerment in the region.

■ **All CAREC countries have committed to the Sustainable Development Goals and to key international gender equality agreements.**

21.   CAREC 2030 supports the SDGs, to which all CAREC countries are also signatories. The achievement of gender equality and women's empowerment is a critical stand-alone goal, articulated through SDG 5, while also being integral to the achievement of all 17 SDGs. Adoption of the SDGs by all CAREC member countries, therefore, represents a common commitment to prioritize gender equality and women's empowerment in national development agendas.

---

[21]   ADB classifies projects into four gender categories: *gender equity* (GEN) is applied to a project if its outcome directly addresses gender disparities; *effective gender mainstreaming* (EGM) is applied to a project if a majority of its outputs directly improve women's access to social services, economic resources, and infrastructure benefits, or enhance women's rights and decision-making; *some gender elements* (SGE) is applied to a project if less than half of its outputs have some direct gender benefits; and *no gender elements* (NGE) is applied to a project if it has only indirect gender benefits (ADB. 2019. *Gender in Infrastructure: Lessons from Central and West Asia*. Manila).

22.   All CAREC countries have ratified the Convention on the Elimination of All Forms of Discrimination against Women[22] and are signatories of the Beijing Declaration and Platform for Action (footnote 17). As United Nations (UN) member states, all CAREC countries have a responsibility to implement the UN Security Council Resolution 1325 on women, peace, and security.[23] Yet, while the majority of the countries have enacted legislation to promote equal rights for women and to prohibit gender-based discrimination, more needs to be done to ensure that these commitments are reflected in plans and policies at the local, national, and regional levels and are properly implemented.

■ **CAREC development partners are committed to advancing gender equality and empowering women.**

23.   Key CAREC development partners view gender equality and women's empowerment as key drivers of economic growth and social development. ADB identifies gender equality as both a critical end goal and as a key driver of sustainable socioeconomic development.[24] Similarly, the Asian Infrastructure Investment Bank sees gender equality as a driver for successful and sustainable economic development and recognizes the need for gender-inclusive and responsive measures in all the projects that it supports.[25] Gender equality is also an integral part of the commitment of the European Bank for Reconstruction and Development to promoting sustainable and environmentally sound development across its investment and donor-funded activities. Equality between men and women is an important development goal for the International Monetary Fund; it also considers women's economic participation as a critical component of growth and stability.[26] Likewise, women's empowerment is a key driver of the Islamic Development Bank's long-term strategic framework.[27] UNDP provides a road map to integrate gender equality into all aspects of its work,[28] while the World Bank views gender equality as central to its goals of ending extreme poverty and promoting sustainable growth.[29]

---

[22]   "The Convention on the Elimination of All Forms of Discrimination against Women, adopted in 1979 by the UN General Assembly, is often described as an international bill of rights for women. It defines what constitutes discrimination against women and sets up an agenda for national action to end such discrimination." (United Nations Entity for Gender Equality and the Empowerment of Women [UN Women]. Convention on the Elimination of All Forms of Discrimination against Women)

[23]   Office of the Special Adviser on Gender Issues and Advancement of Women. Landmark Resolution on Women, Peace and Security (accessed 2 March 2020).

[24]   ADB. 2019. *Strategy 2030 Operational Plan for Priority 2: Accelerating Progress in Gender Equality, 2019–2024*. Manila.

[25]   AIIB. 2019. *Gender Equality for Sustainable Infrastructure*. Panel Discussion during the 2019 Annual Meeting of the AIIB. Luxembourg. 12–13 July.

[26]   International Monetary Fund. Gender and the IMF (accessed 2 March 2020).

[27]   IsDB. 2019. Women's Empowerment Policy. Jeddah.

[28]   UNDP. 2018. *Gender Equality Strategy 2018–2021*. New York.

[29]   World Bank. 2015. *World Bank Group Gender Strategy (FY16–23): Gender Equality, Poverty Reduction, and Inclusive Growth*. Washington, DC.

CHAPTER III

CAREC GENDER STRATEGY APPROACH AND FRAMEWORK

24. The CAREC Gender Strategy articulates the critical importance of ensuring that CAREC interventions improve the lives, livelihoods, and prospects of all people in the 11 CAREC countries and across regions, leaving no one behind. It highlights the gender inequalities that create disadvantages, limit opportunities, and undermine the well-being for women and other vulnerable groups in the CAREC countries. It points to the potential opportunity and human costs of failing to take women's specific needs into account. It also pays attention to the heightened susceptibility of many women and girls to risks from, for example, external events, such as climate-related disasters and pandemics, gender-based violence and harassment, and inadequate access to primary health.

A. Vision

25. The vision of the CAREC Gender Strategy is *"inclusion, empowerment, and resilience for all."* This reflects the critical need (i) to ensure the *inclusion* of women's specific needs and voices at all stages of planning and implementation in regional projects; (ii) to promote the *empowerment* of women through access to capacity building, economic opportunities, and involvement in decision-making; and (iii) to contribute to greater *resilience* for women and their families to minimize risk, promote well-being, and enable sustainable, gender-equitable outcomes.

B. Mission

26. Towards the achievement of the vision, the CAREC Gender Strategy identifies entry points, which should inform the design of CAREC investments and interventions in line with the mission of *"equality and empowerment of women and girls in all CAREC operations for inclusive, shared, and sustainable development."*

C. Regional Approach

27. CAREC's collaborative, regional approach will be instrumental in aligning gender activities among CAREC countries and across CAREC operational clusters to achieve common objectives.

28. To facilitate programmatic planning, implementation, and monitoring of progress in line with the strategy, entry points are organized by strategic gender objectives that are aligned with the five operational clusters of the CAREC 2030 strategy and the SDGs, particularly SDG 5. The entry points are summarized in Chapter IV and elaborated fully in the Appendix.

D. Objectives

29. **Objective 1: Promote women's access to economic opportunities.** Where possible, CAREC interventions will be designed to supplement and add value to national efforts to create opportunities for women to enter paid, formal employment in relevant sectors, support women in agriculture and informal sectors, promote women's entrepreneurship, and allow

women to gain skills that prepare them for jobs in the CAREC sectors. This will include promoting female employment in nontraditional sectors and building women's and girls' capacity in science, technology, engineering, and mathematics (STEM) and in other areas that align with the CAREC labor market needs. It is also important to institute safeguards for female employees and establish minimum standards for employers to guarantee a secure work environment and gender-equitable workplace standards including equal pay. Enabling women to aim for higher incomes through value-added jobs and entrepreneurship opportunities will likewise be supported. The focus will be on reducing sector segregation and narrowing the gender wage gap, nationally and overall, for the CAREC region. Additionally, efforts will be made to assist women in starting or expanding existing MSMEs through the provision of favorable banking products, training in business skills, and other measures.

30.   **Objective 2: Contribute to women's social empowerment.** CAREC interventions will include regional provisions that combine with national strategies to advance gender equality and women's empowerment in terms of:

(i)   Enhancing women's decision-making roles in national institutions and local committees, as well as in CAREC sectors, by ensuring they are well represented in management structures.

(ii)   Reducing women's time poverty through the provision of reliable and affordable infrastructure and supporting measures to reduce unpaid care work (such as workplace day-care facilities, subsidized childcare, and flexible working hours) in order to create opportunities for economic empowerment.

(iii) Taking into account the specific needs, concerns, and perspectives of women, girls, men, and boys to ensure no one is left behind by undertaking effective consultative processes with individuals and groups, including the most vulnerable and those living in remote areas.

(iv)   Promoting women's safety and security and ensuring them no harm as a result of interventions by conducting gender and risk analyses, undertaking safeguarding activities, educating frontline workers and target populations on issues such as harassment and road safety, and ensuring resilience to external shocks, including those due to pandemics such as COVID-19, is built into all planning and programming.

(v)   Strengthening human capital development in education and health across the CAREC countries by fostering knowledge exchange between member countries and connecting women to regional institutes of higher education and centers of excellence to boost their education status and increase their income-earning capacities. The implementation of a regional health strategy will improve regionwide quality healthcare services and access to tertiary hospitals and specialized treatment institutions. Likewise, it will help strengthen surveillance systems and monitoring capabilities across borders to manage the incidence of transmission of infectious diseases, in view of the COVID-19 pandemic.

31.   **Objective 3: Support women's regional networks and policy reform for women's empowerment.** CAREC will support gender-responsive policy reforms, where current legislation is exacerbating gender disparities and creating barriers to women's economic empowerment. CAREC will contribute to an enabling environment for fostering and establishing women's regional networks to promote gender-responsive trade and economic activities, support advocacy for reforms, and enable knowledge- and skills-sharing and cooperation between women in member countries. Regional networks of women will be supported for exchanging knowledge and information across borders on legislative and regulatory regimes for women's empowerment in the various CAREC countries and for enhancing access to information about income-earning and social development opportunities across the region.

32.   **Objective 4: Enhance women's access to information and communication technology.** CAREC interventions will promote better regional digital connectivity by enhancing access of women and men to—and supporting their training in the use of—new digital technologies and affordable ICT solutions. Efforts will be made to support digital services aimed at female entrepreneurs such as business training, information, and online financial access. Such interventions will reduce the connectivity costs across borders and countries, improve competitiveness of small firms and businesses that employ women, and reduce social progress gaps between men and women in the CAREC region.[30]

---

[30]   These objectives were presented and agreed by the countries at the CAREC Consultation Meeting of National Focal Points in Tashkent, Uzbekistan on 24–25 September 2019. Central Asia Regional Economic Cooperation Program (CAREC).

CHAPTER IV

MAINSTREAMING GENDER IN CAREC OPERATIONS
KEY GENDER ENTRY POINTS

33.   This chapter provides strategic guidance for ensuring gender is mainstreamed across all CAREC 2030 program and project decisions, planning, and implementation. The chapter is organized according to the five operational clusters of CAREC 2030, outlining key gender issues and potential strategic directions and entry points for mainstreaming gender into sectors and other priority areas. An additional note is provided regarding ICTs, which is a crosscutting theme across the rest of the clusters. A full list of strategic gender entry points is available in the Appendix. It is important to note that, due to the socioeconomic and cultural diversity of the CAREC countries, decisions will need to be made regarding the prioritization of entry points in individual countries, while the selected entry points will need to be adapted and refined (including setting appropriate targets) for each country context.

A. Economic and Financial Stability Cluster

34.   Macroeconomic policy is often considered gender neutral, benefiting both women and men equally. However, women and men often do not benefit equally from economic growth and fiscal measures designed to boost economies. For example, as outlined in Chapter II of this report, disparities in the Gender Inequality Index (GII) reflect the systematic exclusion of women from lucrative employment opportunities across the CAREC region. The evidence shows that women in all CAREC countries are more likely to be unemployed than men and are often concentrated in the lowest-paid sectors and roles.[31] Women often have problems accessing small loans required for business start-ups or scaling-up of MSMEs because of lack of assets and paucity of appropriate financial products, services, and information in many countries (footnote 12).

35.   Strategic directions for CAREC to mainstream gender into this cluster include the following: (i) promoting equal economic opportunities for women, including in nontraditional jobs and management in both public and private sectors, through policies and strategies; (ii) creating employment standards that promote decent work for all; (iii) complying with international and national legislation on inclusive employment practices; (iv) creating an enabling environment for female entrepreneurs so that they can take full advantage of national programs and new regional economic opportunities in the productive and services sectors, including the promotion of improved financial access and enhanced financial literacy; and (v) building women's and girls' capacity in STEM subjects and ICT to promote their access to emerging areas of employment

---

[31]   Asia Pacific SDG Partnership. SDG Gateway Data Explorer (accessed 15 March 2020).

in CAREC countries. It is vital to inform these strategies with relevant qualitative and quantitative evidence gathered through surveys and consultative processes with female and male beneficiaries, financial providers, and employers. CAREC will also help the countries establish networks for businesswomen's associations from all 11 CAREC countries that will help strengthen cooperation and promote investment opportunities across the region.

36.   CAREC will promote policy dialogue at regional and cross-country levels to enable stakeholders from across the region to learn from each other's experiences and knowledge and put in place best practices for women's empowerment and gender mainstreaming. These include the sharing of countercyclical policy initiatives that take into account the provision of budgetary support to social infrastructure (e.g., for health and education) and to MSMEs headed by women.

37.   CAREC can consider supporting gender-responsive adjustments to the banking sector. These should include better coordinated banking regulations to improve financial inclusion of women and other marginalized groups, supported by regional financial models that promote female entrepreneurship. CAREC will actively engage the private sector to strengthen its commitment to women's economic empowerment through gender-responsive actions that include cross-border investments in agribusiness and tourism.

B. Trade, Tourism, and Economic Corridors Cluster

(i) Trade

38.   Cross-border trading activities for MSMEs and small informal businesses, such as roadside food stalls and guesthouses, account for a significant portion of regional trade in countries along the CAREC corridors and provide a vital source of income for many women. According to estimates from Central Asia and the South Caucasus, supportive measures such as removing supply chain barriers can raise total exports by around 65%, imports by 49%, and gross domestic product by up to 8%.[32] Taking proactive steps to ensure women are included in supply chains, particularly those that inhibit women entrepreneurs in the region, can propel further growth.[33] It is also important to mitigate potentially negative impacts of formalizing border trade, such as harassment or extortion by market and trade officials who may take advantage of the often limited access to information of female traders on market rules.[34]

39.   In order to boost gender inclusiveness across all aspects of trade and create an enabling environment for the economic empowerment of both female entrepreneurs and informal cross-border traders, CAREC, in alignment with the CAREC Integrated Trade Agenda 2030 (CITA), will support the countries in the revision of both national and regional trade policies to include gender-responsive measures. For example, preferential conditions could be introduced for female traders, including the introduction of time-bound subsidies to help women-led export businesses increase their production capacity and market their products in other countries. Financial sector policies should promote incentives for female-owned MSMEs, and government

[32]   World Economic Forum. 2014. Scenarios for the South Caucasus and Central Asia. *World Scenario Series*. Geneva.
[33]   A. Rillo and S. Nugroho. 2016. *Policy Brief: Promoting Agricultural Value Chain Integration in Central Asia and the Caucasus*. Tokyo: Asian Development Bank Institute.
[34]   K. Higgins. 2012. *Gender Dimensions of Trade Facilitation and Logistics: A Guidance Note*. Washington, DC: World Bank.

procurement policies should include supporting the sourcing of goods and services for female-led enterprises. Additionally, agricultural policies should support women farmers to enter and benefit from gender-equitable value chains.

40.   CAREC will facilitate consultations on trade policies with female traders and entrepreneurs across borders to understand their specific needs and the constraints they face. Clear information on important policy changes should be effectively disseminated to female traders. The success of policies and processes in enabling women's economic empowerment should be measured by setting target numbers of female traders and monitoring progress nationally and regionally across CAREC countries.

41.   Trade policies must also ensure that goods have been produced under safe working conditions, free from exploitation, and must include adoption of labor law policies such as work, equal opportunities, and prevention of discriminatory practices (including hiring of women at advanced age). Work practice standards should apply for women working at home. CAREC will enhance information sharing and provide appropriate training for police, border staff, and customs officials to reduce the risk of trafficking, sexual exploitation, gender-based violence, and sexual harassment. Information on preventing sexually transmitted diseases, such as HIV/AIDS, should also be available for predominantly male workers transporting goods, such as lorry drivers.

(ii) Tourism

42.   Globally, women account for 54% of the total workers employed in the tourism industry in areas such as hospitality, informal trading, and handicraft production.[35] Tourism offers many potential opportunities for women, including decent work, entrepreneurship, training, and leadership and decision-making roles. There is great potential to increase women's business and employment in the sector.[36] However, while tourism promotion and open visa regimes have many benefits, these measures can also have unintended consequences, such as increasing or encouraging human trafficking and sexual exploitation.[37] All CAREC countries have enacted legislation against human trafficking and to protect victims.[38] However, more concerted efforts are still needed to tackle this issue in many CAREC countries.[39]

43.   CAREC, in alignment with the CAREC Tourism Strategy 2030, will promote initiatives to ensure women have equal access to information about tourism-related jobs across the region. Support will be provided to CAREC countries to develop regional and cross-country guidelines to ensure that recruitment is based on skills and experience rather than physical appearance, and that women receive gender-equitable pay and have equal access to opportunities such as on-the-job training. The creation of a regional and interconnected tourism market among CAREC countries will generate new opportunities for women of the region, who traditionally have been quite active in the services sector.

---

[35]   UN World Tourism Organization. 2019. *Global Report on Women in Tourism*. 2nd ed. Madrid.

[36]   ADB. 2019. *Promoting Regional Tourism Cooperation under CAREC 2030: A Scoping Study*. Manila.

[37]   Uzbekistan has granted visa-free access to 101 countries starting from July 2018, and Pakistan launched an e-visa scheme for 175 countries in March 2019. The Silk Road visa, a joint initiative between Kazakhstan and Uzbekistan, is also underway (ADB. 2019. *Report and Recommendation of the President to the Board of Directors: Proposed Loan, Technical Assistance Grant, and Administration of Technical Assistance Grant to the Republic of Uzbekistan for the Sustainable Hydropower Project*. Summary Poverty Reduction and Social Strategy [accessible from the list of linked documents in Appendix 2]. Manila).

[38]   Examples include Article 113 of the Criminal Code (Mongolia); Law on Prevention and Combating Trafficking in Persons, 2005 (Kyrgyz Republic); Article 129 of the Criminal Code, 2010 (Turkmenistan); Prevention and Control of Human Trafficking Ordinance and Trafficking in Persons Act, 2018 (Pakistan); and Articles 128, 133, 125(3)(b), 126(3)(b), and 270 of the Penal Code (Kazakhstan).

[39]   For example, four CAREC countries are in Tier 2 of the Trafficking in Person 2019 report watch list for significant efforts but not meeting some of the minimum standards (Azerbaijan, Kazakhstan, the Kyrgyz Republic, and Uzbekistan); while the PRC and Turkmenistan are in Tier 3 for not meeting the minimum standards despite the enactment of laws (United States Department of State. 2019. *Trafficking in Persons Report*. Washington, DC).

44.   CAREC will support specific initiatives to involve women and men from local communities, including those in the border areas, in the planning, development, and operation of tourist attractions and related services to ensure they benefit directly from these initiatives and that profits go back into the community.

45.   Appropriate and proportionate measures must also be taken to address and minimize the risks of gender discrimination, sexual exploitation, sexual abuse, sexual harassment, and trafficking that are sometimes associated with tourism. Taking these issues seriously means ensuring zero tolerance is written into law and implemented by police, border guards, tourist industry leaders, and national and local governments. It also means providing regionwide as well as country-specific targeted information and training for those responsible for implementing anti-trafficking, sexual exploitation, and sexual abuse legislation in the context of tourism. To address this, CAREC will provide regional capacity building programs that will focus on skills building of both women and men regional tourism operators and on private sector tourism businesses to ensure that their corporate policies include gender-sensitive policies.

(iii) Economic Corridors

46.   Economic corridors in the CAREC region provide an effective tool to create business development opportunities, employment, and entrepreneurship, promoting growth through deepened regional cooperation and integration. Economic corridor development involves multisector coordination and multidisciplinary approaches, in particular, private sector investment. The promotion of regional economic corridors will strengthen regional connectivity and create additional income-generating activities for women.

47.   For example, the Almaty–Bishkek Economic Corridor (ABEC) modern wholesale market investment project will create permanent jobs in the marketplace with wholesalers, retailers, exporters, suppliers, enterprises, and farmer cooperatives.[40] Through this and other related initiatives (such as the Trilateral Economic Corridor connecting Kazakhstan, Uzbekistan, and Tajikistan), CAREC will promote initiatives to encourage women to participate in economic corridor activities including cross-border trade and tourism and related services, regional value chain (e.g., agricultural products) development, integrated urban planning, and knowledge sharing and training events.

C. Infrastructure and Economic Connectivity Cluster

(i) Transport

48.   There is a widespread assumption that women and men benefit equally from transport projects and use travel infrastructure in similar ways. However, there are often significant gender differences in transport usage, trip patterns, and mobility constraints in CAREC countries.[41] Women in CAREC countries are less likely to drive and own a vehicle than men. Women are also more likely to use public transport than men for reasons that include commuting to work, attending school and university, and undertaking tasks related to their roles as primary caregivers such as food shopping, taking children to school, and going to clinics. Yet, in many CAREC countries, there is poor access to reliable public transport.[42] When there is access to public transport, it is often too expensive, located too far away, or is considered unsafe: sexual harassment on

---

[40]   ABEC is the pilot economic corridor under the CAREC Program.

[41]   ADB. 2013. *Gender Tool Kit: Transport—Maximizing the Benefits of Improved Mobility for All.* Manila.

[42]   Food and Agriculture Organization of the United Nations (FAO). 2017. *Gender, Rural Livelihoods and Forestry: Socioeconomic and Gender Analysis of the Forestry Sector in Uzbekistan.* Tashkent. pp. 24–26.

public transport has been reported as a growing problem in many CAREC countries.[43] Walking, perhaps along busy roads, therefore, remains the predominant mode of travel for many women, especially in poorer CAREC countries. Roads, though, are often not designed with the pedestrians in mind so that women of all ages, perhaps accompanied by small children, may be obliged to cross several streams of traffic or walk along narrow verges in order to reach their destination. Safety is further compromised at night if lighting is poor.

49.   It is vital that public transport services are convenient, accessible, and safe for all women and children. CAREC, in alignment with the CAREC Transport Strategy 2030, will ensure the provision of affordable services for women and their families to accommodate women's specific travel patterns; promoting gender-sensitive designs that cater to gender-differentiated needs (e.g., with space for baby carriages and separate sections or carriages and ticket offices for women) will likewise increase women's and children's accessibility. CAREC will provide support for collecting gender-disaggregated qualitative and quantitative data for the development of these inclusive solutions at a regional level in the sector.

50.   It is particularly important to integrate measures that address and reduce the risk of sexual harassment and other forms of violence against women when using public transport services connecting countries, given that such cases of harassment have been widely reported as a growing problem in many CAREC countries. CAREC will provide support and training to transport service providers at a regional level in raising awareness on protecting women from sexual and other forms of harassment, aimed at introducing a zero-tolerance policy for any form of sexual harassment, whether verbal or physical, and improving systems for reporting harassment in secure ways. CAREC can also support the launch of information campaigns for transport users and the public to raise awareness about these issues and encourage reporting of perpetrators.

51.   CAREC will provide support to create regional and country-level networks that link transport providers, law enforcement agencies, medical professions, and nongovernment organizations (NGOs) to monitor safety provision and safeguard female transport users through effective reporting and tracking systems.

52.   CAREC will facilitate sharing of knowledge and experiences, and consultations with beneficiaries, to understand the specific needs of women and men when designing both main and feeder roads for better accessibility and improved safety for all. Adequate lighting must be provided along routes to bus stops or local villages to make women and other vulnerable groups visible to oncoming traffic and to make them less susceptible to threats such as theft or sexual harassment (footnote 10). The provision of suitable walkways, pedestrian bridges, and bus shelters are crucial in ensuring accessibility, comfort, and safety. Mandatory road safety measures and clear signage are also important for (often male) drivers and pedestrians in the CAREC countries. Additionally, accessible gender-sensitive and marginalized-inclusive amenities—such as spaces for diaper changing and breastfeeding, where possible, and toilets and service stops for persons with disabilities—must also be provided for both women and men on major transport routes.

53.   CAREC will support member countries in developing regional and national-level policies and guidelines to increase employment opportunities for women in the transport sector, going beyond the stereotypical roles in administration and encouraging their application for technical and managerial roles in road and rail transport, aviation, and logistics. This means making the application process for employment in transport firms gender-sensitive and more transparent. It also means encouraging girls to study STEM subjects that will prepare them for technical roles, as well as providing on-the-job training and regional and country cluster-level training programs. Setting targets for female

43   ADB. 2015. *Policy Brief: A Safe Public Transportation Environment for Women and Girls*. Manila.

employees and managers in the transport sector will enable progress in women's economic empowerment to be tracked.

(ii) Energy

54.   Energy poverty is a part of the broader economic poverty and has clear gender dimensions. Women generally manage the energy use of the household and are, therefore, directly and often adversely affected by the lack of clean and efficient energy sources.[44] Energy poverty has an impact on women and girls due to the toll it takes on their time, especially since they are primarily responsible for collecting fuel or preparing stoves for cooking and domestic heating. This impacts their quality of life and any potential for economic empowerment. Women and children's health is also more likely to be negatively affected by poor air quality in homes due to burning biofuels.[45] An improved, more efficient, and environmentally sustainable energy supply can have positive health outcomes and implications for economic empowerment, freeing up time for women to seek employment or engage in other economic activities (footnote 45).

55.   Energy provision should take into account women's needs so they have access to affordable, targeted services. This means ensuring that all aspects of energy service design are grounded on gender-sensitive evidence gathered. For this, CAREC can facilitate consultative processes and surveys. CAREC will seek to strengthen and inform regional energy policies that promote positive social and environmental impacts, with a focus on reducing domestic energy costs to increase access of poorer households (including those that are headed by women) and providing low-cost carbon-neutral energy options.

56.   CAREC can support the creation and improvement of national and regional information systems to generate sex-disaggregated data on issues such as accessibility, affordability, and income generation to inform transport and energy planning. CAREC will enable learning between CAREC countries through, for example, regional exchanges between government ministries, private sector companies, female energy sector professionals, and NGOs.

57.   CAREC will actively support initiatives in the growing green energy market at the regional level, which could provide a useful source of employment for women. For example, economic opportunities can be created for women in the emerging green energy sector by training them in technology and sales for renewable energy products such as solar lamps.[46] It is also important to create opportunities for women to take up technical and professional posts with energy suppliers. CAREC will also support the introduction of policies that foster equal opportunities in traditional energy sectors, including generation, transmission, and distribution. At the regional and cross-country levels, CAREC will enable partnerships between regional energy suppliers, universities, and technical and vocational education and training (TVET) institutions to provide professional development for women in energy-related operations and maintenance.

---

[44]   UN Women and World Bank. 2018. *Policy Brief 12: Global Progress of SDG 7—Energy and Gender*. Accelerating SDG 7 Achievement. Washington, DC.

[45]   ADB. 2012. *Gender Tool Kit: Energy—Going Beyond the Meter*. Manila.

[46]   In Pakistan, the Agency for Technical Cooperation and Development (ACTED) launched a pilot project to promote sustainable solutions for women's empowerment, providing technical training in solar energy. With support from ADB, ACTED trained 54 women in Multan, Punjab as solar technicians (ADB. 2018. Solar Energy Training Brightens up Employment Opportunities for Pakistan's Women. Video. 8 March).

58.   The strategies above will complement the CAREC Energy Strategy 2030, which includes "Empowering Women in Energy" as a crosscutting theme.[47] To increase women's visibility in the sector, the strategy foresees the establishment of a regional women's energy program to improve their careers and make them more employable. Likewise, setting up regional networking and support facilities is also envisioned.

D. Agriculture and Water Cluster

(i) Agriculture

59.   Both the agriculture sector and society would benefit significantly from closing the gender gap in this sector. Yields on farms could increase by 20%–30% if women had the same access to productive resources as men. An estimated 43% of women globally work in agriculture. This percentage greatly varies among the CAREC countries. In Afghanistan, for example, women in agriculture make up 82.0%, closely followed by the PRC (64.0%) and Pakistan (56.9%); while, in other CAREC countries, the percentage remains as low as 6.8% in Kazakhstan and 11.7% in Georgia.[48]

60.   However, work in the agriculture sector is often poorly paid or even unpaid. Waged employment comprises only a small share of women's involvement in agriculture, and they are more likely to participate as contributing unpaid family workers.[49] In some CAREC countries, women perform manual labor, such as in food processing and packaging, and other value-added activities.[50] Gender power asymmetries mean that women often lack control of assets and have restricted access to finance and information, as well as low participation in commercial and export-oriented markets.[51] This undermines the economic potential of women in agriculture.

61.   Closing the gender gap in agriculture requires multiple actions at policy and practical levels. CAREC will promote the development of both regional and country-level approaches to promote gender-equitable access to credit, agricultural extension services, and digital technologies such as mobile phones and apps connecting them to market pricing information and potential buyers. Ongoing activities conducted by CAREC in the agriculture sector include (i) training and participation of women in sanitary and phytosanitary safeguards and standards to promote higher safety standards, including through the establishment of a regional food safety network; and (ii) development of regional wholesale markets, which will provide bigger avenues for women farmers to market their produce and earn additional income by engaging in cross-border trade. The CAREC Gender Strategy 2030 will complement these activities and strengthen gender mainstreaming through, for example, capacity building for women farmers on new agricultural practices and technologies, which will contribute to creating regional agricultural value chains.

(ii) Water Management

62.   In the CAREC countries, women often have the primary responsibility for the household's water management and are, thus, disproportionately burdened by water supply and quality issues. Access to clean, running water within the household on a regular basis can make a huge difference in women's lives, reducing their time poverty and improving quality of life for them and their families. They are also significantly impacted by flooding and waterborne diseases.

---

[47]   ADB. 2019. *CAREC Energy Strategy 2030*. Manila.
[48]   FAO. 2011. *The State of Food and Agriculture 2010–11—Women in Agriculture: Closing the Gender Gap for Development*. Rome.
[49]   T. Khitarishvili. 2016. *Gender Inequalities in Labour Markets in Central Asia*. New York: UNDP.
[50]   ADB. 2020. *Vegetable Production and Value Chains in Mongolia*. Manila.
[51]   See available ADB Country Gender Assessments on CAREC countries for more information.

63.   With the increased labor migration of men in many CAREC countries, women have begun to take on a greater role in agriculture, including in water resources and irrigation management.[52] However, women often have limited representation in water user associations, partly because inequitable laws prevent them from being registered landowners.[53]

64.   CAREC will facilitate women's participation in regional mechanisms for transboundary water resources management and increase women's representation in responses to emergencies to address impacts on food and water security and water and sanitation infrastructure. It will also assist in strengthening regional disaster risk management and reducing climate change-related risks, which will likewise improve women's security and resilience in the region.

65.   The growing water sector in many CAREC countries is also a potential source of well-paid employment for women, not only in administrative but also in technical and managerial roles. CAREC can help in establishing mechanisms to recruit women into technical and managerial roles in the water sector and in providing on-the-job trainings for them to participate more effectively in regional water projects.

E. Human Development Cluster

(i) Education

66.   The majority of CAREC countries have achieved gender parity or near parity in primary and secondary education. However, the clear exceptions are Pakistan, where nearly 50% more boys than girls have received a secondary education; and Afghanistan, where girls only account for around a third of secondary school students.[54]

67.   Despite the growing number of women with secondary and tertiary education in many CAREC countries, they still lag far behind in STEM subjects.[55] Gender norms and perceptions strongly influence female students' chosen field of study in the CAREC countries.[56] Strengthening human capital development in education across the CAREC countries will help to connect women in the region to institutes of higher education and technical trainings to boost their education status and increase their income-earning capacities.

68.   CAREC will actively promote better alignment of women's educational choices with employment opportunities nationally and across the CAREC region. The program will support the development of strategies at the regional and intercountry levels that could include partnering with national and regional TVET providers to offer courses—including on digital platforms—in sectors relevant to the CAREC project areas, with emphasis on training women in nontraditional skills such as plumbing, carpentry, electrical work, and machine operation. CAREC can also consider providing scholarships and other incentives for girls and women in STEM and other technical subjects to help offset the risks of early dropout.

---

[52] S. Balasubramanya. 2018. Why Women are Key for Water Management in Tajikistan. *Farming First*. 5 July.

[53] For example, a 2013 study found that only 18% of water user association members in the Kyrgyz Republic were women (UNDP. 2013. *Climate Profile of the Kyrgyz Republic*. Bishkek).

[54] A 2012 report found that dropout rates among girls in Afghanistan were considerably higher—i.e., 31% for girls while only 13% for boys (Samuel Hall Consulting. *School-in-a-Box 2015 Evaluation*, commissioned by the Womanity Foundation [accessed 2 March 2020]).

[55] For example, in Kazakhstan, men accounted for 100% of enrolment in electrical engineering and transport technology during the academic year, 2011–2012 (footnote 1).

[56] For example, in Georgia, only around a quarter of women are studying engineering, manufacturing, and construction, but they comprise 80% of arts and humanities students and 70% of those studying health at tertiary level (footnote 10).

CAREC will support efforts of national governments to address cultural norms and biases that undermine girls' education and to raise awareness on the importance of educating girls.

69.   Steps should be taken at the regional and country levels to increase women's representation in management and decision-making of schools and universities, including TVET institutions.

(ii) Health

70.   There has been a steady improvement across health indicators in the CAREC countries; nonetheless, there is continued poor access to health services in some countries, particularly those ranked as having *low* or *medium* human development in the UNDP Human Development Index. It is also likely that several gains in health sector improvement in the CAREC countries will have been undermined by the global COVID-19 pandemic. Maternal mortality ratios are relatively low in a majority of the countries, with the exception of Afghanistan, where 396 maternal deaths per 100,000 live births were registered in 2015, followed by Pakistan with 178.[57] Evidence indicates that targeted investments can make a marked difference to health outcomes.[58]

71.   CAREC will support the countries in developing a regional health strategy that will, among other things, help strengthen surveillance systems and monitoring capabilities across borders for control of communicable and noncommunicable diseases, and improve access of women and men to quality medicines at more affordable costs across the region.

72.   CAREC can also add value by exploring and sharing knowledge on new technologies and digital solutions, such as cross-border tele-health and e-health services, which will enhance access, particularly of women who have constrained mobility, to quality medical advice nationally and across border regions in neighboring countries. Promoting equitable access to these digital services has become even more urgent in light of the COVID-19 pandemic.

73.   Cross-country exchange of affordable and innovative technologies for promoting women's health—including maternal health care, addressing sexual and reproductive health issues such as family planning, combating sexually transmitted diseases, and eliminating unsafe abortions—and the provision of services to remote, underserved areas will be encouraged. Regional preparedness for crises, such as pandemics, should also be enabled through the creation of a gender-inclusive regional public health emergency response strategies and risk communications.

74.   CAREC will also provide support to improve access to health services for migrant female workers and health professionals in the region, for example, through targeted training programs to improve their skills and facilitate their movement.

---

[57]   This can be compared with Kazakhstan at the other end of the scale, with only 12 maternal deaths per 100,000 births (footnote 7).

[58]   Institute for Health Metrics and Evaluation. Global Health Data Exchange. Global Burden of Disease Study 2017 (GBD 2017) Data Resources. GBD Results Tool (accessed 20 February 2020). For example, after investing considerably in improvements to maternal health, Azerbaijan decreased its maternal mortality ratios from 47 maternal deaths per 100,000 births in 2000 to 25 deaths in 2020 (footnote 49). In addition, Azerbaijan's average life expectancy rose from 66.8 years in 2000 to 72.9 years in 2018 (UNDP. 2019. Briefing Note for Countries on the 2019 Human Development Report: Azerbaijan. New York).

F. Information and Communication Technology

75.   The importance of digital technology is becoming increasingly evident across the world, particularly in light of the COVID-19 pandemic. ICT is providing an invaluable resource for businesses in the form of e-commerce and virtual communications, as well as for access to education, health, and other vital services. Improving access to ICT is a crosscutting issue for CAREC 2030, with critical gender dimensions that are reflected in Objective 4 of this strategy. There is a digital divide in the CAREC countries, where women lag behind men in access to digital technology.[59] This means that female entrepreneurs miss the opportunities that digital platforms offer for improving access to finance, increasing economic participation, and accelerating business growth (footnote 19).

76.   CAREC can help close the gender gap in digital access. For example, through the conduct of regional trainings and workshops, CAREC can build capacity in ICT for women and girls of all ages, particularly in the CAREC countries where the gender gap is widest.

77.   Women and girls are often at most risk from cyber bullying and exploitation by sexual predators. Regional strategies to mitigate these risks must be developed, implemented, and closely monitored to avoid any potential harm.

78.   CAREC will support the creation of regional or intercountry partnerships with private sector digital providers for the provision of internet access to poor households and remote, rural communities across countries; develop the capacity of women in practical digital technologies; and provide training in digital technologies for female students and employed women. CAREC will actively engage the private sector ICT companies to participate in these schemes through sponsoring intercountry and regional initiatives.

79.   CAREC will also promote the creation of regional knowledge networks to share good, gender-sensitive practices for enhancing women's access to ICT and increasing their opportunities in information technology-related employment.

---

[59]   A. Demirgüç-Kunt, L. Klapper, D. Singer, S. Ansar, and J. Hess. 2018. *The Global Findex Database 2017: Measuring Financial Inclusion and the Fintech Revolution*. Washington, DC: World Bank.

CHAPTER V

INSTITUTIONAL AND IMPLEMENTATION ARRANGEMENTS

80. The CAREC Gender Strategy 2030 will be aligned with national strategies while supplementing and adding value to national efforts on gender mainstreaming to best achieve women's empowerment in the region. It will be implemented through the CAREC sector strategies and action plans, providing strategic guidelines and directions for effectively mainstreaming gender in their operations.

81. The CAREC Secretariat will coordinate the implementation of the CAREC Gender Strategy. Three clear mechanisms aligned with the CAREC 2030 Institutional Framework will be established: (i) a Regional Gender Expert Group (RGEG) that will provide strategic guidance and expert inputs, as and when needed, for the strategy's effective implementation; (ii) enhanced collaboration between the CAREC Secretariat, member countries, development partners, and the CAREC Institute; and (iii) a monitoring and evaluation mechanism, which will facilitate tracking and communication of results across the CAREC region on the implementation of the strategy.

82. **Regional Gender Expert Group.** Coordinated by the CAREC Secretariat, the RGEG will comprise of representatives from all CAREC member countries and interested development partners. Nominees to the RGEG could include representatives from the women's ministries, national-level committees, academia, and the media as well as gender focal points of the ministries of economy and key CAREC sector ministries. In addition, representation from national and international civil society and international NGOs within the region may

be sought. The RGEG will closely collaborate with the CAREC sector focal points and committees to ensure effective implementation of the strategy. The RGEG scope of work will include developing a regional gender action plan, monitoring its implementation, providing guidance and support to mainstreaming gender in sector-specific projects, and designing gender stand-alone initiatives, among others. The RGEG will convene at least once a year to review progress on implementation of the strategy.

83. **Enhanced collaboration between the CAREC stakeholders.**

(i) **CAREC member countries.** The CAREC Secretariat will work with the member countries to ensure high-level ownership of the CAREC Gender Strategy 2030 and its implementation. Under the leadership of the CAREC national focal points (NFPs), regional cooperation coordinators and advisors to the NFPs will support effective engagement with country-based stakeholders, experts, women's associations, and other existing structures, such as the national commissions, to enable and track gender mainstreaming activities, including data collection and reporting.

(ii) **Development partners.** The CAREC Secretariat will seek the support and expertise of development partners, including close collaboration with the gender experts of ADB. Regional peer-to-peer learning exchanges and knowledge sharing will be sought using digital platforms, where expedient.

(iii) **Mainstreaming gender in the CAREC Institute's research.** The CAREC Secretariat will coordinate with the CAREC Institute on policy dialogue and knowledge sharing, including the development of CAREC-specific knowledge products on gender. The RGEG will form part of the peer review panel for these knowledge products.

84. **Implementation arrangements.** Following the endorsement of the strategy, the CAREC Secretariat will request the NFPs for nomination to the RGEG and identify gender focal points in governments of the member countries. Member of the RGEG for each country will ensure internal coordination with various stakeholders. The CAREC Secretariat, in collaboration with these gender experts, will develop a first draft of the RGEG's terms of reference. Once the CAREC RGEG focal points have been appointed, terms of reference for the RGEG will be finalized through the inception meeting.

85. **Monitoring and evaluation mechanism.** The CAREC Gender Strategy 2030 results framework has been developed to assess progress in the implementation of the strategy. For each of the five operational clusters, with an additional section on ICTs, it states the expected outputs that aim at achieving specific outcomes for each of the four proposed objectives and contribute to the impact. The CAREC Secretariat will closely work and communicate with the CAREC sector focal points and committees to track progress on sector strategies and feed them into this monitoring mechanism. Necessary tools like the Gender Information System can be developed in support of the monitoring mechanism.

CHAPTER VI

CAREC GENDER STRATEGY 2030 RESULTS FRAMEWORK

86.   The CAREC Gender Strategy 2030 results framework (Table 2) demonstrates the results chain, stating the expected outputs and the desired outcomes for each operational cluster and for each defined objective. The projected outcomes and outputs will contribute to the overall impact of inclusion, empowerment, and resilience for all in the CAREC region. The results framework will help member countries and the CAREC Secretariat monitor progress of the CAREC Gender Strategy 2030.

87.   No target indicators are provided at this stage. The CAREC Secretariat will closely work with the sector committees, working groups, and proposed RGEG to feed sector strategies into this mechanism and develop concrete cluster and sector-specific gender indicators. Every 3 years, the CAREC Secretariat will prepare a consolidated progress report by taking stock of progress on the gender results framework.

Table 2: CAREC Gender Strategy 2030 Results Framework

IMPACT	Inclusion, Empowerment, and Resilience for All in the CAREC Region			
OUTCOMES	**1. Women's access to economic opportunities promoted** *Barriers to labor force participation removed, enabling environment for female entrepreneurship created, occupational stereotypes dismantled, number of management and leadership positions occupied by women in CAREC sectors increased, and gender wage gaps closed in CAREC sectors.*	**2. Social empowerment of women increased** *Gender gaps narrowed, resulting in women's economic and political empowerment, greater access to productive resources and opportunities, and improved quality of life for women in the CAREC countries.*	**3. Women's regional networks and policy reform supported for women's empowerment** *Gender-responsive policy reforms supported, and enabling environment for fostering and establishing women's regional networks created.*	**4. Women's access to ICT increased** *Women's and girls' access to ICT and ICT literacy improved in the CAREC countries.*
OUTPUTS	**A. Economic and Financial Stability**			
	Targets for female employees and for training of women in technical areas included in CAREC projects. Female entrepreneurs supported through measures that include preferential interest rates and business training. Banking regulations to improve financial inclusion of women and other marginalized groups supported by regional financial models that promote female entrepreneurship.	CAREC projects' design based on information from consultations with women and men, and implementation regularly reviewed to ensure it continues to meet the specific needs of women and men. Training in gender sensitivity in place for all CAREC employers, employees, and funders.	Regional and cross-country policy dialogue and research to promote policy reform that removes structural impediments to women's participation in economic activities enhanced. Women's capacity to advocate for their economic and social empowerment, and awareness of rights increased.	Female entrepreneurs' access to appropriate ICT enhanced. Training in software and platforms for technical support, online sales, and business-focused information provided. Initiatives introduced to increase access of female entrepreneurs to affordable digital financial services.
	B. Trade, Tourism, and Economic Corridors			
	Preferential conditions introduced for female traders, including the introduction of subsidies for female-led export businesses. Systems in place for mapping progress in increased economic empowerment of female traders, nationally and regionally, across the CAREC countries.	Trade, tourism, and economic policies informed by consultations with female traders, and quantitative evidence informed equally by female and male traders. Regional and country-level policies and measures in place to ensure that goods have been produced under safe working conditions, free from exploitation or harassment.	National and regional trade policies revised to include gender-responsive measures. Finance policies promote financial and nonfinancial incentives for the private sector and female-led MSMEs. Policies and measures in place, reducing bottlenecks for female cross-border traders.	Expand women's access to digital technologies, enabling them to access digital tourism platforms and expand their market. Improved access to ICT infrastructure, services, and digital literacy for women and girls.

continued on next page

Table 2: *Continued*

OUTPUTS	B. Trade, Tourism, and Economic Corridors *(continued)*			
	Information exchange networks in place for female traders to share and distribute market, pricing, and other information. Workplace guidelines and policies in place to ensure that recruitment is based on skills and experience rather than on physical appearance, and that women receive gender-equitable pay and have equal access to opportunities such as on-the-job training. Systems established at CAREC country and regional levels to collect and analyze gender-disaggregated tourism-related data.	Training in gender sensitivity in place for police, border staff, and customs officials to reduce the risk of trafficking, sexual exploitation, and sexual harassment in border areas. Regionwide and country-specific targeted information and training available for those responsible for implementing anti-trafficking, sexual exploitation and sexual abuse legislation in the context of tourism. Regional capacity building programs introduced for private sector tourism businesses to ensure that their corporate policies include gender equality measures.	Government procurement policies support the sourcing of goods and services from female-led enterprises. Gender-responsive national economic and development policies and frameworks in place and implemented in the CAREC countries. Regional policy forums activated. Systems and processes for CAREC intercountry knowledge sharing on gender-responsive best practices in place. Women's capacity to advocate for their economic and social empowerment, and awareness of rights increased. Gender support and advocacy networks established at national and regional levels.	Provision of accessible and affordable internet and digital platforms to women, particularly in the poorest CAREC countries. Support to women-led digital start-ups and increase in their number.
	C. Infrastructure and Economic Connectivity			
	Regional and national-level policies and guidelines established to increase employment opportunities for women in transport and energy, going beyond the stereotypical roles in administration and encouraging their application for technical and managerial roles. Increased number of girls studying STEM subjects in the CAREC countries. All CAREC transport and energy projects include targets for female employees and for training of women in technical areas such as engineering.	Measures in place to ensure the specific needs of women and men are met in road and energy design so they can access and benefit from them fully and safely. All aspects of transport and energy service design grounded on gender-sensitive evidence gathered from women through consultative processes and surveys. National and regional information systems created to generate sex-disaggregated data on issues such as accessibility, affordability, and income generation to inform transport and energy planning.	Reforms at national and regional levels to ensure energy policies promote positive social and environmental impacts, with a focus on making access to energy affordable to vulnerable households. Regional and/or country clusters technical training programs in place for female staff and those interested in working in technical areas of the energy and transport sectors.	

continued on next page

Table 2: *Continued*

OUTPUTS				
C. Infrastructure and Economic Connectivity *(continued)*				
	Target number of women trained in technical and managerial roles, technology, and sales of renewable energy products such as solar lamps.

Policies fostering equal opportunities in established energy sectors introduced.

Systems and processes for CAREC intercountry knowledge sharing on best gender-responsive practices in place. | Measures in place that address and reduce the risk of sexual and other forms of harassment of women using public transport, including training for transport providers on protecting women from sexual harassment; introducing zero-tolerance policies for any form of sexual harassment, and public awareness-raising.

Regional and country cluster-level networks created to share knowledge, monitor safety provision, and safeguard female users.

Women's time poverty reduced through the introduction of labor-saving technologies, access to modern energy infrastructure, and others. | Regional and cross-country networks, databases, and learning exchanges in place for sharing best practices and innovative approaches to support employment and professional growth of women in the energy and transport sectors. | |
| **D. Agriculture and Water** | | | | |
| | Women farmers better integrated into domestic and regional supply chains for agriculture and agribusiness.

Women farmers have equal access to credit, agricultural extension services, and digital technologies such as mobile phones and apps connecting them to market pricing information and potential buyers.

Provisions to improve agricultural extension support and access to productive resources such as land, seeds and water, and improved access to markets for women farmers. | Affordable and accessible water and sanitation services provided for all.

The needs of women and their families are understood and met by engaging them in the service design process through grassroots consultations and surveys. | Women involved as active participants in regional mechanisms for transboundary water resources management.

Women equally represented in cross-country or regional-level responses to emergencies to address impacts on food and water security and water and sanitation infrastructure.

Regional and cross-country networks, databases, and learning exchanges in place for sharing best practices and innovative approaches to support employment and professional growth of women in the agriculture and water sectors. | Women farmers have access to digital technology and platforms such as mobile phones and mobile apps to share knowledge, contact potential buyers, and share information about market prices of agricultural goods.

Increased use of technologies (including ICT) to reduce women's time poverty and improve access to formal labor markets. |

continued on next page

Table 2: *Continued*

D. Agriculture and Water *(continued)*			
Intercountry agricultural value chain channels in place for female producers and agricultural entrepreneurs, supported by the development of digital platforms and apps to promote gender-sensitive cross-border agricultural trade. All CAREC water projects include targets for recruiting women into technical and managerial roles in the water sector and providing on-the-job training. Systems and processes for CAREC intercountry knowledge sharing on best gender-responsive practices in place.			
E. Human Development			
Regional standards in place to increase women's participation in higher education, including in STEM subjects. Increased opportunities for women in higher education, and technical and vocational training, particularly in nontraditional occupations. Regional and intercountry level partnerships with national and regional TVET providers established in sectors relevant for CAREC project areas, particularly in nontraditional skills such as plumbing, carpentry, electrical work, and machine operation. Scholarships and other incentives provided for girls and young women in STEM and other technical subjects.	Increased number of women is represented in management and policy making in schools and universities. Basic health services provided for women and children in CAREC project areas. Women trained and employed in regional efforts to address disease control and public health.	Gender-responsive regional public health emergency response strategy in place for the CAREC countries. Regional and cross-country networks, databases, and learning exchanges in place for sharing gender-responsive best practices and innovative approaches to health and education.	Remote areas reached through tele-health, e-health services, and other ICT solutions, and accessible by women. Mechanisms established for enabling cross-country exchange of affordable and innovative technologies for maternal healthcare.

OUTPUTS

continued on next page

Table 2: *Continued*

	F. Information and Communication Technology			
OUTPUTS ↑	E-commerce promoted for female-led businesses, and digital capacity of female entrepreneurs increased by at least 40%.	Funds allocated to support the provision of affordable and accessible internet-enabled mobile phones and subsidized internet to poor women in the CAREC countries. Increased women's and girls' capacity in ICT through targeted training. Strategies to improve cybersecurity introduced and closely monitored at regional and national levels.	Regional or intercountry partnerships created with private sector digital providers to support the provision of internet access to poor households and remote, rural communities; develop the capacity of women in practical digital technologies; and provide training in digital technologies for female students and employed women.	

CAREC = Central Asia Regional Economic Cooperation; ICT = information and communication technology; MSMEs = micro, small, and medium-sized enterprises; STEM = science, technology, engineering, and mathematics; TVET = technical and vocational education and training.

Source: Asian Development Bank.

FULL LIST OF STRATEGIC GENDER ENTRY POINTS

A. Economic and Financial Stability Cluster

Objective 1: **Promote women's access to economic opportunities.**

- ☐ Set employment standards that promote decent work for women and men in public institutions and private companies within Central Asia Regional Economic Cooperation (CAREC) sectors.
- ☐ Conduct studies to assess the impact of business laws on women entrepreneurs and informal cross-border traders, and build capacities for disaggregated data collection and management for an integrated regional labor market information system.
- ☐ Integrate gender equality into the design and development of a CAREC Financial Inclusion Strategy.
- ☐ Launch Gender Impact Bonds as an instrument for CAREC 2030-related interventions and projects, implemented with mandatory Sustainable Development Goals and gender results to qualify as a success.[1]
- ☐ Develop guides on business and taxation laws, regulations, and procedures in all CAREC countries, with a focus on addressing the issues and concerns of women entrepreneurs and businesswomen's associations.
- ☐ Set CAREC-wide regional targets for business loans provided to women entrepreneurs and encourage lenders to establish special credit lines with lower interest rates or additional benefits, such as business training.
- ☐ Ensure that female entrepreneurs have access to relevant, targeted, affordable business training, as well as dedicated business development support programs and mechanisms (from incubation to business expansion and financing) for female-led micro, small, and medium-sized enterprises (MSMEs) and female entrepreneurs.
- ☐ Ensure female traders have equal access to trade finance, financial technology such as e-commerce platforms, and events such as trade fairs.
- ☐ Support cross-border private sector investments in agriculture, agribusiness, and tourism to support women's entrepreneurship.
- ☐ Support home-based employment of women in the outsourcing sector as measure to mitigate impacts that the coronavirus disease (COVID-19) has had on women who have to stay at home for care duties.

Objective 2: **Contribute to women's social empowerment.**

- ☐ Include women in national and regional policy development and decision-making on financial sustainability and macroeconomic policy.
- ☐ Encourage cross-border private sector involvement in education, health, and other service sectors that increases women's participation and improves the quality of services.

---

[1] Impact bonds combine the capital of different actors, especially the private sector, in diverse ways to raise new finance with a focus on development results. It is a complicated undertaking and should be piloted only in countries where the government is fully on board. Careful selection is also important as payments are upon impact and initial payouts will determine whether such instruments fail or succeed.

☐ Ensure women are able to benefit from social safety net programs to protect them from shocks, such as the COVID-19 pandemic, which may result in reduced working hours due to increased childcare responsibilities or to job loss given women's less secure formal or informal employment.

Objective 3: **Support women's regional networks and policy reform for women's empowerment.**

☐ Create opportunities for cross-country dialogue and sharing of countercyclical policy measures that include budgetary support to social infrastructures (e.g., health and education) and to female-led MSMEs.

☐ Establish cross-country forums to exchange experiences and lessons on improving women's access to loans.

☐ Put in place better coordinated banking sector regulations that improve financial inclusion for women and other marginalized sectors.

☐ Establish regional financial models that bolster MSME financing and support women's entrepreneurship.

☐ Establish regional networks for businesswomen's associations from all 11 CAREC countries to strengthen cooperation and explore investment opportunities.

Objective 4: **Enhance women's access to information and communication technology.**

☐ Enhance female entrepreneurs' access to appropriate information and communication technology (ICT) and support training in software and platforms for technical support, online sales, and business-focused information.

B. Trade, Tourism, and Economic Corridors Cluster

Objective 1: **Promote women's access to economic opportunities.**

☐ Sensitize corporate procurement to MSMEs' needs and create provisions in corporate procurement guidelines to support women-owned and -managed MSMEs.

☐ Set targets for capacity building of agency personnel to increase understanding of trade-related gender issues.

☐ Train women traders and support them in navigating government requirements and processes regulating cross-border trade.

☐ Build and support information exchange networks for female traders to share and distribute market, pricing, and other information using mobile phones.

☐ Include women in traders' associations, producer networks, cooperatives, and other professional networks along the supply chain for goods and services identified for different economic corridors.

☐ Ensure the collection and analysis of gender-disaggregated data on tourism at the CAREC regional and country levels, with statistics provided systematically by hotels and other tourist-related establishments. For this purpose, tourism institutions in each country should establish a proper registry, cadastre, and operating licenses for all business activities and enterprises of the tourism sector, including digital platforms of home stays and bookings. There should also be an inspection body to verify the accuracy of information provided.

Objective 2: **Contribute to women's social empowerment.**

☐ Involve women and men from local communities in the planning, development, and operation of cross-border tourist attractions and related services to ensure they benefit directly from these initiatives.

☐ Support the introduction or reinforcement of measures and a zero-tolerance policy to reduce the risk of gender discrimination, sexual exploitation, and harassment of women, girls, and boys in areas of increased regional tourism and cross-border trade routes.

☐ Introduce regional capacity building programs for private sector tourism businesses to ensure that their corporate policies include gender equality measures (ensuring equal opportunities for career progression, equal hourly rates, etc.).

Objective 3: Support women's regional networks and policy reform for women's empowerment.

☐ Develop regional forum of women entrepreneurs involved in cross-border trade at the regional level.

☐ Create multicountry capacity building programs for women entrepreneurs with regard to policy and legal frameworks of trade and tourism.

☐ Create multicountry challenge fund for young entrepreneurs to enable them to launch new MSMEs.

☐ Support the development of gender-responsive trade policies at regional and country levels that encourage increased recruitment of female employees and buying of goods and services from female entrepreneurs, and which support women farmers' inclusion in value chains.

☐ Establish regional trading policies and tariffs to ensure that goods traded equitably benefit the producers and have been produced under safe working conditions, free from exploitation.

☐ Ensure that customs and integrated trade facilitation include women-friendly border crossing points and logistics facilities, customs simplification and harmonization, and web-based information catering to specific needs of women traders.

☐ Set up and support women's regional tourism networks and tourism cooperatives to access and benefit from investments made in tourism promotion under CAREC. Link women's tourism networks to similar global networks to explore new markets through women-to-women connections.

Objective 4: Enhance women's access to information and communication technology.

☐ Expand women's access to digital technologies and training in their use, enabling them to promote their goods and services through e-commerce and expand their markets across borders.[2] This is an urgent measure given the disproportionate impact of COVID-19 on women and the associated global increase in online sales.

C. Infrastructure and Economic Connectivity Cluster

Objective 1: Promote women's access to economic opportunities.

☐ Adopt policies on equal opportunities to increase the number of women hired and trained in technical and professional posts in the energy and transport sectors, and promote technical, vocational, and on-site training.

☐ Support female entrepreneurs in the energy and transport sectors by allocating special quotas in investment funds of local, national, and regional financial institutions.

☐ Consider the needs of women in planning for economic activities around stations and on roadsides, and promote economic opportunities for women (e.g., reserved retail spaces in railway stations for female-owned businesses).

☐ Explore digital solutions for women producers, traders, and other female transport users (e.g., through ride-sharing apps for coordinated transport and cost-sharing).

---

[2] The Kyrgyz Community-Based Tourism Association can be taken as a good example on how to successfully use ICTs to create economic opportunities for women. The Association created business opportunities for women in rural and remote areas where there is no access to the internet but where people have mobile phones. (ADB. 2014. *Information and Communication Technologies for Women Entrepreneurs: Prospects and Potential in Azerbaijan, Kazakhstan, the Kyrgyz Republic, and Uzbekistan.* Manila.)

- Create economic opportunities for women in the emerging green energy sector by training them in technology and sales for renewable energy products, such as solar lamps.
- Support the creation of partnerships between utilities providers, universities, and technical and vocational education and training (TVET) institutions to provide training for women students in science, technology, engineering, and mathematics (STEM) and relevant TVET programs; and professional development programs for women in operations and maintenance as well as in management.
- Develop multicountry skill development courses with regional certification to promote high standards and consistency across CAREC countries.

Objective 2:   Contribute to women's social empowerment.

- Include designs sensitive to gender-differentiated needs and needs of persons with disabilities, and universal access features for public transport including buses, subways, and overland trains (e.g., ensuring buses and train carriages have spaces for parking baby carriages and have accessible entrance ways).
- Identify women's preferences in the design, installation, and use of renewable energy technologies, especially at the household and community levels.
- Increase awareness among decision-makers about gender issues related to transport and energy.
- Provide free or affordable credit for energy supply to support poor and/or households headed by women by reducing their time poverty and improving air quality in their homes.
- Establish effective mechanisms for addressing grievances in a timely manner, and collating and analyzing information relating to complaints.
- Improve national and regional information systems to generate sex-disaggregated data on issues such as accessibility, affordability, and income generation to inform transport and energy planning.
- Ensure transport service providers receive training in protecting women from sexual harassment and introducing a zero-tolerance policy from any form of sexual harassment, whether verbal or physical.
- Create CAREC network and country cluster networks of nongovernment organizations (NGOs), police and/or law enforcement, medical service providers for establishment of a network of help desks and/or kiosks, and helplines to ensure the safety of all (especially the vulnerable) in the streets and in transport systems.

Objective 3:   Support women's regional networks and policy reform for women's empowerment.

- Develop regional energy trade policies that take into account poverty, social, and environmental benefits, and which (i) reduce domestic energy costs to enable greater access to energy by poor households, including households headed by women; and (ii) promote the acquisition of renewable energy to provide poor households, including those headed by women, with choices on energy sources.
- Develop regional policies and/or guidelines to promote the increased employment of women in national railway, road, aviation, logistics, and infrastructure agencies.
- Design regional and/or country cluster technical training programs for women staff and applicants in railway, road, aviation, and logistics infrastructure operations and maintenance.
- Establish regional and cross-country networks and learning exchanges on best practices and innovative approaches to support employment and professional growth of women in railways, road transport, aviation, and logistics infrastructure among private sector companies, national government agencies, academe, and women professionals.

- Establish a network of women's groups, NGOs, and/or civil society organizations; private sector; government utilities; financial institutions; and universities and TVET institutions to (i) develop capacities of women in communities (especially female heads of households) to become producers and consumers of clean energies ("prosumers"),[3] and (ii) support women to access green finance and/or use green technologies in their businesses and/or households.
- Promote cross-country and/or regional learning exchanges among private sector companies, women energy professionals, entrepreneurs, and community leaders on the development of new clean energy technologies and/or innovative use of clean energy technologies for business, household use, and community development.
- Ensure the collection of gender-disaggregated data at the CAREC country levels to inform inclusive transport solutions, as well as the implementation of gender impact assessments to assess progress against these indicators.

D. Agriculture and Water Cluster

Objective 1: Promote women's access to economic opportunities.
- Increase the participation of women in water supply operations by training them as (paid) water pump operators, maintenance workers, and managers.
- Ensure women farmers have access to agricultural extension services.
- Support the development of new technologies on food or agribusiness production and climate change adaptation beneficial to women's agricultural productivity.
- Promote regional approaches to strengthen women's access to land and financial services in agribusiness.
- Open intercountry agricultural value chain channels for women producers and entrepreneurs.
- Promote the expansion of traditional and digital platforms for cross-border agricultural markets in support of women's employment and gender-inclusive business climate.

Objective 2: Contribute to women's social empowerment.
- Conduct gender sensitization training for the agriculture sector stakeholders in government, local agencies, and businesses.
- Integrate women's perspectives as landowners, water users, household water managers, and representatives of water and agriculture sectors into the design, operation, and maintenance of water systems.
- Ensure women have access to mechanisms for resettlement and grievance resolution.
- Support and expand women-managed water user associations (WUAs) and ensure women's equal representation in existing WUAs to improve community water management practices.
- Support reforms to increase land ownership of women.
- Develop public–private governance mechanisms for household water supply networks with the participation of women.
- Ensure governance of urban water supply and sanitation is gender-responsive and informed by the needs of female and male users.

Objective 3: Support women's regional networks and policy reform for women's empowerment.
- Build and support information exchange networks for female growers and farmers to share and distribute market pricing and other information, using mobile phones and other digital platforms.
- Support gender-equitable policy reform in land ownership.

---

[3] Office of Energy Efficiency and Renewable Energy. 2017. *Consumer vs. Prosumer: What's the Difference?* 11 May.

- ☐ Create intercountry capacity development programs for women on new agricultural practices, agricultural technologies, and value chain activities compliant to global standards.
- ☐ Develop regional standards on water, sanitation, and hygiene distribution that ensure women's access to water for irrigation, kitchen plots, and household needs.
- ☐ Promote women's representation in regional mechanisms for transboundary water resource management.
- ☐ Ensure women are represented in responses to emergencies to address impacts on food systems and water, sanitation, and hygiene infrastructure.
- ☐ Rejuvenate and extend the Gender and Water Network (GWANET) to all CAREC countries to ensure that the policy debate on water at the regional, national, and local levels is gender sensitive.

Objective 4: Enhance women's access to information and communication technology.
- ☐ Ensure women farmers have access to digital technology and platforms such as mobile phones and mobile apps to share knowledge, contact potential buyers, and share information about market prices of agricultural goods.

E. Human Development Cluster

Objective 1: Promote women's access to economic opportunities.
- ☐ Partner with national and regional TVET providers to offer courses, including on digital platforms, in sectors relevant to the CAREC project areas, with emphasis on recruiting and training women in nontraditional skills such as plumbing, carpentry, electrical work, and machine operation.
- ☐ Support scholarships for girls and women in STEM and other technical subjects.
- ☐ Ensure leadership training and skills are included in school curricula for girls and young women.
- ☐ Promote work between the CAREC countries for the collection and joint analysis of sex-disaggregated data to track gender-differentiated patterns of access to health care and health outcomes.

Objective 2: Contribute to women's social empowerment.
- ☐ Develop regional standards among higher education institutions to increase women's participation, including in nontraditional TVET courses and STEM subjects.
- ☐ Promote women's representation in policymaking and management of TVET and STEM education.
- ☐ Conduct regional and national scoping studies to identify and prioritize women's knowledge, training, and health needs in the CAREC project areas.
- ☐ Set up basic health units to meet the needs of women, men, and children in the CAREC countries, particularly in remote and underserved areas. Ensure there is adequate capacity and equipment to support good maternal and infant health.
- ☐ Launch education and awareness campaigns on the importance of vaccination, basic sanitation, and other public health issues.
- ☐ Promote cross-country exchange of affordable innovative technologies for maternal health protection and delivery of other social services to remote and underserved areas.

Objective 3: Support women's regional networks and policy reform for women's empowerment.
- ☐ Create intercountry initiatives for higher education, such as student exchange programs for female students in nontraditional TVET and STEM courses.

- ☐ Ensure equal access of women and girls to (gender-sensitive) information on health and health services for prevention and treatment. Support exchange of knowledge, best practices, and health promotion materials within and between CAREC countries.
- ☐ Develop intracountry strategies to protect the most vulnerable residing in border areas (women, the elderly, children, persons with disabilities, and migrant and mobile populations and their intersections) from disease outbreaks and improve their access to health services.
- ☐ Facilitate cross-country exchange of affordable innovative technologies for maternal health protection and delivery of other social services to remote and underserved areas.
- ☐ Enable intercountry leadership development for women in policymaking and management of public health concerns.
- ☐ Ensure that a gender-inclusive regional public health emergency response strategy is in place.

Objective 4: Enhance women's access to information and communication technology.
- ☐ Introduce e-learning for women in priority areas, such as remote regions.
- ☐ Explore possibilities to introduce tele-health and e-health services in the more remote areas.
- ☐ Promote intercountry leadership development for women in policymaking and management of public health concerns.

F. Information and Communication Technology (Crosscutting Entry Points)

- ☐ Support capacity building in ICT for women and girls of all ages, including in schools and higher education institutions. Ensure teachers are properly trained and equipment is available and up to date.
- ☐ Support the provision of affordable and accessible mobile phones or other digital platforms for women and other vulnerable groups, especially in the CAREC countries where mobile phone ownership is low.
- ☐ Develop cross-country or regional education policies and programs to support poor and rural women's access to ICT technical and/or practical education through provision of scholarships and vocational–technical training by universities and TVET institutions.
- ☐ Support the provision of subsidized or free internet, with a focus on reaching women and other vulnerable groups in the CAREC countries.
- ☐ Explore the potential of ICT as a means to increase women's access to finance, health, and information on agricultural prices and other areas in the CAREC countries to inform planning.
- ☐ Support regional learning exchanges on the creation of opportunities for women's employment and business development using ICT.
- ☐ Establish regional or intercountry partnership agreements with the private sector for any or all of the following: (i) provision of Wi-Fi and internet access in rural and poor communities; (ii) capacity development of women in poor and rural communities on practical technologies, technological applications for their learning and livelihood, and employment; (iii) provision of funds and/or ICT materials and equipment for use in the development of women's businesses; and (iv) provision of on-the-job training and employment for women graduates of STEM courses and relevant vocational–technical programs, as part of the corporate social responsibility thrusts of private companies.
- ☐ Establish regional programs to provide incentives to private sector companies with initiatives to support women's access to ICT for education and/or business development.
- ☐ Set up regional learning exchanges on good practices on creation of opportunities for women's employment and business development using ICT.
- ☐ Create a CAREC database of gender-responsive best practices in all the CAREC sectors that is widely accessible for all the CAREC stakeholders and (potentially) beneficiaries.

BIBLIOGRAPHY

Asia Pacific SDG Partnership. SDG Gateway Data Explorer (accessed 15 March 2020).

Asian Development Bank (ADB). 2012. *Gender Tool Kit: Energy—Going Beyond the Meter*. Manila.

———. 2013. *Gender Tool Kit: Transport—Maximizing the Benefits of Improved Mobility for All*. Manila.

———. 2014. *Gender Tool Kit: Micro, Small, and Medium-Sized Enterprise Finance and Development*. Manila.

———. 2014. *Information and Communication Technologies for Women Entrepreneurs: Prospects and Potential in Azerbaijan, Kazakhstan, the Kyrgyz Republic, and Uzbekistan*. Manila.

———. 2015. *Policy Brief: A Safe Public Transportation Environment for Women and Girls*. Manila.

———. 2016. *Pakistan: Country Gender Assessment. Volume 1 of 2: Overall Gender Analysis*. Manila.

———. 2016. *Pakistan: Country Gender Assessment. Volume 2 of 2: Sector Analyses and Case Studies*. Manila.

———. 2016. *Tajikistan: Country Gender Assessment*. Manila.

———. 2017. *CAREC 2030: Connecting the Region for Shared and Sustainable Development*. Manila.

———. 2017. Project Report: Consolidated Report on Gender Expertise of PFIs under ADB Women's Entrepreneurship Development Project. Manila.

———. 2018. *Georgia: Country Gender Assessment*. Manila.

———. 2018. *Kazakhstan: Country Gender Assessment*. Manila.

———. 2018. *Report and Recommendation of the President to the Board of Directors: Proposed Loan to the Republic of Uzbekistan for the Horticulture Value Chain Infrastructure Project*. Summary Poverty Reduction and Social Strategy (accessible from the list of linked documents in Appendix 2). Manila.

———. 2018. *Report and Recommendation of the President to the Board of Directors: Proposed Loan and Grant to the Kyrgyz Republic for the Climate Change and Disaster-Resilient Water Resources Sector Project*. Summary Poverty Reduction and Social Strategy (accessible from the list of linked documents in Appendix 2). Manila.

———. 2018. Solar Energy Training Brightens Up Employment Opportunities for Pakistan's Women. Video. 8 March.

———. 2018. *Uzbekistan: Country Gender Assessment—Update*. Manila.

———. 2019. *Azerbaijan: Country Gender Assessment*. Manila.

———. 2019. *CAREC Energy Strategy 2030*. Manila.

———. 2019. *CAREC Integrated Trade Agenda 2030 and Rolling Strategic Action Plan 2018–2020*. Manila.

———. 2019. *Gender in Infrastructure: Lessons from Central and West Asia*. Manila.

———. 2019. *Kyrgyz Republic: Country Gender Assessment*. Manila.

———. 2019. *Promoting Regional Tourism Cooperation under CAREC 2030: A Scoping Study*. Manila.

———. 2019. *Report and Recommendation of the President to the Board of Directors: Proposed Grant and Administration of Grant to the Islamic Republic of Afghanistan for the Arghandab Integrated Water Resources Development Project*. Summary Poverty Reduction and Social Strategy (accessible from the list of linked documents in Appendix 2). Manila.

———. 2019. *Report and Recommendation of the President to the Board of Directors: Proposed Loan to the Republican State Enterprise Kazvodkhoz for the Irrigation Rehabilitation Project (Guaranteed by the Republic of Kazakhstan)*. Summary Poverty Reduction and Social Strategy (accessible from the list of linked documents in Appendix 2). Manila.

———. 2019. *Report and Recommendation of the President to the Board of Directors: Proposed Loan, Technical Assistance Grant, and Administration of Technical Assistance Grant to the Republic of Uzbekistan for the Sustainable Hydropower Project*. Summary Poverty Reduction and Social Strategy (accessible from the list of linked documents in Appendix 2). Manila.

———. 2019. *Strategy 2030 Operational Plan for Priority 2: Accelerating Progress in Gender Equality, 2019–2024*. Manila.

———. 2019. *Technical Assistance for Sustainable Tourism Development in the Central Asia Regional Economic Cooperation Region*. Manila.

———. 2020. *Vegetable Production and Value Chains in Mongolia*. Manila.

ADB and International Labour Organization (ILO). 2011. *Women and Labour Markets in Asia: Rebalancing for Gender Equality*. Bangkok: ILO Regional Office for Asia and the Pacific.

Asian Infrastructure Investment Bank (AIIB). 2019. *Gender Equality for Sustainable Infrastructure*. Panel Discussion during the 2019 Annual Meeting of the AIIB. Luxembourg. 12–13 July.

Balasubramanya, S. 2018. Why Women are Key for Water Management in Tajikistan. *Farming First*. 5 July.

Brody, A., J. Demetriades, and E. Esplen. 2008. *Gender and Climate Change: Mapping the Linkages – A Scoping Study on Knowledge and Gaps*. Brighton: BRIDGE/Institute of Development Studies.

Central Asia Regional Economic Cooperation Program (CAREC). CAREC Consultation Meeting of National Focal Points in Tashkent, Uzbekistan on 24–25 September 2019 (accessed 2 March 2020).

Demirgüç-Kunt, A., L. Klapper, D. Singer, S. Ansar, and J. Hess. 2018. *The Global Findex Database 2017: Measuring Financial Inclusion and the Fintech Revolution*. Washington, DC: World Bank.

Food and Agriculture Organization of the United Nations (FAO). 2011. *The State of Food and Agriculture 2010–11—Women in Agriculture: Closing the Gender Gap for Development*. Rome.

———. 2015. The Role of Agricultural Innovation Systems in Central Asia and Caucasus Countries and China towards More Sustainable Food Security and Nutrition. Summary Proceedings of Online Discussion at the Global Forum on Food Security and Nutrition in Europe and Central Asia.

———. 2016. *Gender and Rural Development in Eastern Europe and Central Asia: Key Issues*. Rome.

———. 2017. *Gender, Rural Livelihoods and Forestry: Socioeconomic and Gender Analysis of the Forestry Sector in Uzbekistan*. Tashkent. pp. 24–26.

GSMA (Global System for Mobile Communications Association, originally Groupe Spécial Mobile). 2019. *Connected Women: The Mobile Gender Gap Report 2019*. London.

Heintz, J. and A. Glyn. 2015. Why Macroeconomic Policy Matters for Gender Equality. *Policy Brief No. 4*. New York: United Nations Entity for Gender Equality and the Empowerment of Women (UN Women).

Higgins, K. 2012. *Gender Dimensions of Trade Facilitation and Logistics: A Guidance Note*. Washington, DC: World Bank.

Imankulova, B. N. and K. O. Dzhusupov. 2018. Some Issues of Occupational Health of Health Care Workers in Central Asia (Review). *Annals of Global Health*. 84(3). pp. 459–464.

Institute for Health Metrics and Evaluation. Global Health Data Exchange. Global Burden of Disease Study 2017 (GBD 2017) Data Resources. GBD Results Tool (accessed 20 February 2020).

International Finance Corporation. 2017. *MSME Finance Gap: Assessment of the Shortfalls and Opportunities in Financing Micro, Small, and Medium Enterprises in Emerging Markets*. Washington, DC.

International Monetary Fund. Gender and the IMF (accessed 2 March 2020).

Islamic Development Bank (IsDB). 2019. *Women's Empowerment Policy*. Jeddah.

Japan International Cooperation Agency (JICA) and INTEM Consulting, Inc. 2013. *Country Gender Profile: Mongolia*. Ulaanbaatar: JICA Mongolia Office.

JICA and Samuel Hall. 2013. *Country Gender Profile: Afghanistan*. Kabul: JICA Afghanistan Office.

Khan, T. and A. Monazza. 2013. *Mongolia: Gender Disparities in Labor Markets and Policy Suggestions*. Washington, DC: World Bank.

Khitarishvili, T. 2016. *Gender and Employment in South Caucasus and Western CIS*. New York: United Nations Development Programme (UNDP).

———. 2016. Gender Dimensions of Inequality in the Countries of Central Asia, South Caucasus, and Western CIS. *Levy Economics Institute. Working Papers Series No. 858*.

———. 2016. *Gender Inequalities in Labour Markets in Central Asia*. New York: UNDP.

Kim, E. 2019. Sustainability of Irrigation in Uzbekistan: Implications for Women Farmers. In P. T. Chandrasekaran, ed. *Water and Sustainability*. London: IntechOpen Limited.

Memon, J. A., B. Cooper, and S. Wheeler. 2019. Mainstreaming Gender into Irrigation: Experiences from Pakistan. *Water*. 11(11). p. 2408.

Mongolian Gender Equality Center. 2017. *General Situations and Attitudes on Sexual Harassment Intimidation and Abuse against Women and Girls in the Workplace: Comparative Analysis 2004 and 2017*. Ulaanbaatar.

Mukhamedova, N. 2018. *The Sweet and Bitter Truths about Women in Agrarian Central Asia*. CGIAR Research Program on Water, Land and Ecosystems. Montpellier: Consultative Group on International Agricultural Research.

Office of the Special Adviser on Gender Issues and Advancement of Women. Landmark Resolution on Women, Peace and Security (accessed 2 March 2020).

Paul, S. and V. Sarma. 2013. Economic Crisis and Female Entrepreneurship: Evidence from Countries in Eastern Europe and Central Asia. *Discussion Papers 13/08*. Nottingham: University of Nottingham/Centre for Research in Economic Development and International Trade (CREDIT).

Rillo, A. and S. Nugroho. 2016. *Policy Brief: Promoting Agricultural Value Chain Integration in Central Asia and the Caucasus*. Tokyo: Asian Development Bank Institute.

Samuel Hall Consulting. *School-in-a-Box 2015 Evaluation*, commissioned by the Womanity Foundation (accessed 2 March 2020).

Singh, R. 2017. *Central and South Asia: Disconnected in the Digital Age*. Presentation for Digital Central Asia South Asia (CASA) Programme. Sixth Session of the Asia–Pacific Information Superhighway (AP–IS) Steering Committee. Dhaka. 1–2 November.

Skinner, E. 2011. *Gender and Climate Change: Overview Report*. BRIDGE Cutting Edge Pack on Gender and Climate Change. Brighton: Institute of Development Studies.

Sustainable Mobility for All. 2017. *Global Mobility Report 2017: Tracking Sector Performance*. Washington, DC: World Bank.

Turakhanova, D. 2019. *Gender Equality in Higher Education and Vocational Education and Training in Central Asia: Trends and Challenges*. European Union Programme for Central Asia. Central Asia Education Platform Phase II (CAEP 2).

Twum, J. et al., eds. 2019. *Listen to Her: Gendered Effects of the Conflict over Nagorno-Karabakh and Women's Priorities for Peace*. Tbilisi, Georgia: Kvinna till Kvinna Foundation.

United Nations. 2020. *Policy Brief: The Impact of COVID-19 on Women*. New York. 9 April.

United Nations Development Programme (UNDP). Human Development Reports. Gender Inequality Index (accessed 2 March 2020).

——. 2013. *Climate Profile of the Kyrgyz Republic*. Bishkek.

——. 2018. *Gender Equality Strategy 2018–2021*. New York.

——. 2019. Briefing Note for Countries on the 2019 Human Development Report: Azerbaijan. New York.

United Nations Entity for Gender Equality and the Empowerment of Women (UN Women). Convention on the Elimination of All Forms of Discrimination against Women (accessed 2 March 2020).

——. The Beijing Platform for Action Turns 20 (accessed 2 March 2020).

UN Women and World Bank. 2018. *Policy Brief 12: Global Progress of SDG 7—Energy and Gender*. Accelerating SDG 7 Achievement. Washington, DC.

United Nations World Tourism Organization (UNWTO). 2019. *Global Report on Women in Tourism*. 2nd ed. Madrid.

United States Agency for International Development (USAID). 2019. Crossing Rivers. News and Information. 26 July.

United States Department of State. 2019. *Trafficking in Persons Report*. Washington, DC.

World Bank. Enterprise Surveys (accessed August 2020).

——. 2006. Gender Equality as Smart Economics: A World Bank Group Gender Action Plan (Fiscal Years 2007–10). *Working Papers*. Washington, DC.

——. 2015. *World Bank Group Gender Strategy (FY16–23): Gender Equality, Poverty Reduction, and Inclusive Growth*. Washington, DC.

——. 2016. *Project Paper on a Proposed Additional Loan in the Amount of $140 Million to the Republic of Azerbaijan and Restructuring for a Third Highway Project*. Washington, DC.

——. 2017. *Project Appraisal Document on Proposed Credits in the Amount of US$169.135 Million and a Proposed Grant in the Amount of US$56.565 Million Equivalent to the Republic of Tajikistan for a Nurek Hydropower Rehabilitation Project – Phase I*. Washington, DC.

——. 2018. Kyrgyz Republic: Third Phase of the Central Asia Regional Links Program Project. *Project Appraisal Document*. Washington, DC.

World Economic Forum. 2014. Scenarios for the South Caucasus and Central Asia. *World Scenario Series*. Geneva.